You Are Beautiful

Unlocking Beauty from Within

Rosalind Y. Tompkins

Strategic Book Publishing

Copyright © 2010

All rights reserved – Rosalind Y. Tompkins

No part of this book may be reproduced or transmitted in any form or by any means, graphic, electronic, or mechanical, including photocopying, recording, taping, or by any information storage retrieval system, without the permission, in writing, from the publisher.

Scripture quotations are from the King James Version, the New American Standard Translation, or the New International Versions of the Bible.

Hebrew and Greek definitions are from *The New Strong's Exhaustive Concordance of the Bible*.

English definitions are taken from *Webster's Encyclopedic Unabridged Dictionary* and *Merriam-Webster's Collegiate Dictionary, Tenth Edition*.

Original poetry is written by Rosalind Y. Tompkins.

Strategic Book Publishing
An imprint of Strategic Book Group
P.O. Box 333
Durham CT 06422
www.StrategicBookGroup.com

ISBN: 978-1-60911-363-6

Printed in the United States of America

Book Design: Suzanne Kelly

ENDORSEMENTS

Once again, author Rosalind Tompkins displays her rare anointing, and the gifting of the Most High God as she exercises her poetic talent in her newest book, *You Are Beautiful*. As you read *You Are Beautiful*, you will be transported on eagle's wings and hind's feet to the high places, where, as you dwell in the secret place of our God and His Christ, you will be healed and refreshed. In addition, as you bask in His presence, you will receive beauty for ashes and become a reflection of God's glory; and you will be strengthened to go forth in His Spirit, to be all He has called you to be.

I would like to say how very proud I am of Rosalind, my spiritual daughter, and to commend her for allowing the Lord to use her. May those who read this book receive healing, deliverance, and a Divine impartation of the glory of the Lord.

Bishop Dr. Shirley Holloway Washington D.C.

As I began reading *You Are Beautiful*, I immediately began to rejoice in my spirit that finally someone is putting into print the truth about what every woman struggles with, that is, the question, "Am I really beautiful?"

Rosalind Tompkins not only understands where we as women are coming from in our daily struggle with our feelings about beauty, but she has been graced with an incredible ability to reveal the truth about what real beauty is and how to attain it!

I believe that as you embark on the journey of uncovering your true beauty with Rosalind in *You Are Beautiful*, you will find yourself laughing, crying, and being set free from the chains that society has ensnared you with in regard to what beauty really is. And out of that you will discover that indeed you are beautiful!

Pastor Ruth Chironna
Orlando, FL

Riveting, inviting, inspirational, and passionate, Rosalind Tompkins has done it again—touched the heart and soul from her heart and soul. *You Are Beautiful* is a masterpiece with divine purpose, and the poems are spiritually uplifting.

Brenda Jarmon, PhD, MSW
Associate Professor, Florida A&M University

Pastor Tompkins, in this must-read book, speaks to the deepest core of every woman; and she unmasks the ever running fountain of beauty so divinely given to each woman.

Co-Pastor Judy Mandrell
Life Changers COGIC, Inc. Tallahassee, FL

Awesome description of knowing you are beautiful, because God said it. Rosalind's expression of beauty from a biblical perspective is life changing!

Renae Rollins-Dees
Licensed Hair Technician/Founder
World Class Academy of Beauty

Thank you, Pastor Rosalind, for your words of inspiration, affirmation, and encouragement. I was blessed with greater knowledge and understanding of who I am in Christ. God made me special, unique and BEAUTIFUL!

Bonita Hampton

Dedication and Acknowledgements

I dedicate this book first and foremost to the Lord Jesus Christ, whom I could not have written this book without! He saved, delivered, and revealed true beauty to me, and I am eternally grateful. Also, I dedicate this book to my daughter, Janar; my granddaughter, Tayla; and all the beautiful young ladies that they represent. In addition, I dedicate this book to all the women of God everywhere, no matter what age, race, color, size, or stature. Finally, this book is written in memory of the most beautiful woman of all, my mother, the late Louise Clark, in remembrance always of her smile, which lit up my life and the lives of others!

A Mother's Love

A Mother's love is sent from above;
Created by God to show how it's done,
It nurtures, it heals, it covers, and it fills;
It possesses and caresses,
Just like the One and Only Begotten Son.
It is unconditional love that is sent from above,
From God our Father who is also a Mother.
The closest thing that I have ever seen
To the real deal of love that is like none other
Is manifested in God in the person of a Mother!

Table of Contents

	Introduction.. xi
	Poetry Break—"You Are Beautiful"........................ xiii
1	What Is Beauty?..1
	Poetry Break "You Are"..9
2	Beauty for Ashes...11
	Poetry Break "I Am the Joy"............................15
3	Beautiful Feet..17
	Poetry Break "Destiny's Calling".....................21
4	Ageless Beauty 23
	Poetry Break "I Remember"..............................34
5	Sex Is Beautiful...35
	Poetry Break "Marriage"...................................39
6	Clothed in Beauty 41
	Poetry Break "Greatness" 45
7	Beautiful Wounds...47
	Poetry Break "Destiny Fulfilled"......................50
8	Uniquely Beautiful...51
	Poetry Break "Dream Again"............................55
9	Beautiful Health..57
	Poetry Break "Where Is Hope?".......................65

10	Kingdom Beauty	67
	Poetry Break "I Cannot Be Shaken"	70
11	Beauty Transformation	71
	Poetry Break -"Transformation"	78
12	Beauty Affirmations	79
	Poetry Break "Can We Talk?"	82
13	The Beauty of Wisdom	83
	Poetry Break "Powerful"	90
	"Water & Sand"	91
	Poems of Africa	93

Introduction

I was riding in the car several years ago with my then nineteen year old daughter, Janar, when she began to talk about youth and beauty. I must admit that I had to hold my tongue and listen to her perspective because I knew that it was a pivotal opportunity to get inside her head. She started talking about how she felt as an upcoming sophomore in college. She stated that there would be younger and prettier girls coming on campus and she and her friends were getting older and thus less attractive to the young men because they were no longer freshmen and "fresh meat," so to speak. She also revealed her fear of her boyfriend's losing interest in her as a result. As she talked, I kept sneaking side glances of my beautiful daughter, who was maturing nicely into a young woman, but still very much my baby girl! It was at that moment that I remembered the truth of the saying that "Beauty is in the eye of the beholder." I assured my daughter that she was still very much a young, vibrant, beautiful young lady. After we parted, I wondered if she really heard me.

Have you ever had a day when you felt like a toad? Maybe you woke up late and couldn't get your hair to lie straight, and your favorite outfit was too tight to wear because of the desserts that you had been eating. Or maybe you looked in the mirror and wondered about the aging stranger looking back at you, thinking, How did she get in there? If you can relate to what I am talking about, then this book is for you. We all have days and sometimes seasons when we feel downright ugly inside and out. *You Are Beautiful* will help you navigate through those times. I

Rosalind Y. Tompkins

will endeavor to answer the question, What is beauty? We will look at beauty according to God's perspective, which is found in His word, the Holy Bible. We will look at tangible ways to feel good inside and out even if you aren't a size two and you don't look like a Hollywood model! I have also included original poetry throughout the book, and we will take poetry breaks designed to inspire the beauty in you.

You Are Beautiful

Beauty resides in the hearts of those who seek to find it.
I am often reminded of how it eludes those who think it is hidden.
When truth be told, it is all around us waiting to be uncovered and discovered from within.
Beauty is present to bring pleasure that we can treasure throughout the ages as we turn the pages of our lives.
Why does beauty seem to hide behind images that are fleeting and fading and often wading in hypocrisy and lies?
It is often disguised by what appears to be real.
The only problem is that when it is captured, it leaves you hollow and full of sorrow and regret.
Beauty that is only skin deep is not beauty at all because true beauty is found well below the surface, and it resides in the very core of one's soul.
Truth be told, beauty that is felt is beauty that is seen, and true beauty is found in everything.
It is in the trees, in the sky, and especially in the eyes of those filled with God's presence.
Beauty must be cherished and pampered, loved and acknowledged; or it will be malnourished and forget its purpose and die a slow death.
Beauty is as beauty does because life is not only measured by how you look, but by who you are and by what you do. And I must say to you that ***You are Beautiful!***

CHAPTER 1

What Is Beauty?

Unlocking Beauty from Within!

The question of beauty has been debated throughout the ages. It is timeless in its ability to generate heated discussions with passionate feelings. Beauty, according to *Webster's Encyclopedic Unabridged Dictionary*, is "the quality that is present in a thing or person giving intense pleasure or deep satisfaction to the mind; an attractive, well-formed girl or woman; a beautiful thing, as a work of art, building, etc." In Psalm 139:13-14 the Bible states: "For you created my inmost being, you knit me together in my mother's womb. I praise you because I am fearfully and wonderfully made; your works are wonderful, I know that full well."

Wonderful (it actually states wonderfully in the Strong's Concordance for the translation) is the Hebrew word *palah* \ paw· law\; and it means "to be distinct, be marked out, be separated, be distinguished." God made us to be different, and that is where the beauty lies. There is no one else exactly like you on planet earth. When God made you, He broke the mold. That's the essence of your beauty, your uniqueness! God didn't create you to imitate others. He created you to be one of a kind, distinctively you. There is no one size fits all in beauty. That's why I say to you right now, *"You are beautiful!"* No matter your race, size, hair color, hair length, the color of your skin, shape, age, or what you are wearing, *you are beautiful* because God made you; and He doesn't make junk.

Society's stereotypical thinking has created an unrealistic idea of beauty to sell products. Too many people have bought the lies and sold them to our children throughout the generations. Countless women have self-hatred because of the lies about beauty. They really believe that they are ugly or somehow don't measure up. We will talk more about this subject in Chapter 8, "Uniquely Beautiful." Now we will look at three clichés surrounding beauty, "Beauty is as beauty does," "Beauty is only skin deep," and "Beauty is in the eye of the beholder," in order to gain wisdom and insight and to help answer the question, "What is beauty?"

"Beauty is as beauty does."

Beauty is as beauty does is a saying that has been passed down for many generations. I was first introduced to it by my mother as a young girl because I was always getting into trouble at school. I didn't quite understand it at the time because after all, I reasoned in my young mind, what did my looks have to do with my getting into trouble? Much later in life I began to see the wisdom in this saying. I realized that I could have on my prettiest dress with ribbons in my hair to match and shiny patent leather shoes; but if I pinched my fellow classmates or talked incessantly while the teacher was trying to give a lesson, or fought little boys after school, then my behavior did in fact make me ugly. No matter how dressed up I was, my actions overshadowed my beauty.

Today, I can see that truth all around—not just in children, but in adults as well. So many times we go to church, work, or some other event dressed in our best clothes, clean from head to toe, but won't speak to someone because of a real or perceived offence. When we gossip about the neighbors, our family, our boss, our pastor, or even our friends and argue and fuss with our loved ones, we become ugly, no matter how nice we may look, because our actions do indeed affect our appearance. I have met countless beautiful and handsome people who were made ugly by their attitude and actions. Just because they had been blessed with a pleasant or beautiful outer appearance, they felt that it gave them a license to be arrogant, mean, or manipulative. I have heard beautiful people say things like, "I can get away with anything because, look at me, all I have to do is bat my eyes and everyone will do what I want." They actually believe that and live like that! It's often because others have allowed them to become "spoiled" based upon their looks. However, I have come to the realization that when one behaves in that manner, then that diminishes true beauty and becomes manipulation and control.

Psalm 149:4 states, "For the LORD taketh pleasure in his people: he will beautify the meek with salvation. (KJV) The word "beautify" in Hebrew is, *pa'ar*\ paw· ar\, and it means "to glorify, beautify, adorn." The word "meek" in Hebrew is, *anayv*\ aw· nawv\, and it means "poor, humble, afflicted, meek, needy, weak, lowly." God beautifies based upon our disposition, which affects our actions. A humble or lowly attitude will cause God to pour out His glory and thus make you truly beautiful, no matter what your outer appearance may be.

Another way that "beauty is as beauty does" is based upon good works. Mother Theresa was an example of someone who purposefully lived a life of strict moderation due to a vow of poverty. The pictures that we see of her are by no stretch of the imagination glamorous; but those familiar with Mother Theresa's unselfish work in Calcutta, India, with extremely poor lepers and the establishment of leper colonies all over the world, will have to agree that her good works made her a beautiful person; and so can yours.

The Bible states in Matthew 5:14, "You are the light of the world. A city set on a hill cannot be hidden; nor does anyone light a lamp and put it under a basket, but on the lamp-stand, and it gives light to all who are in the house. Let your light shine before men in such a way that they may see your good works, and glorify your Father who is in heaven." (NASB) This speaks to the whole concept of obedience, because we must become obedient to God's desire for us to be a light. Obedience is what produces good works, and good works cause one to be a light in the midst of darkness, to shine with beauty from God. The opposite of that is true as well: disobedience to God leads to dead works and results in ugliness. If you are feeling ugly on a particular day, make a concerted effort to help someone. Do a good deed for someone in need and watch how your beauty rises from within. As you become the light of this world, shine on!

"Beauty is only skin deep."

In today's society we are bombarded by images in music videos of women who are half naked and dancing lewdly with gyrating hips. The men are depicted as thugs, with gold jewelry and foul mouths, who drive big cars with much "bling, bling." Oftentimes the song lyrics consist of ways to have sex while spewing derogatory words about women. No wonder young ladies are confused about what constitutes real beauty.

"Beauty is only skin deep" is a saying that I believe gets to the heart of where beauty comes from. It implies that for some, beauty begins with the outward appearance and stays there. Beauty that is only skin deep is not beauty at all, because a pretty face, hair, and body, or nice clothes are all surface attractiveness, with no depth. That kind of beauty fades with age and life circumstances. That is why women are getting cosmetic plastic surgery at increasingly younger ages. There are talk shows depicting girls as young as seventeen years of age desiring and oftentimes getting plastic surgery to change their appearance to avoid the aging process. The truth is that beauty is more than skin deep. True beauty comes from within and is seen outwardly. One might say, But I want to look good and sexy in order to find my man; how can inward beauty help me? The answer to that question can be found in the word of God. In the Bible in 1 Peter 3:3-4, it states, "Whose adorning (Greek word *kosmos* \ kos ·mos\—"the world, the universe") let it not be that outward adorning (Greek word *kosmeo* \ kos· meh ·o\—"to put in order, arrange, make ready, prepare) of plaiting the hair, and of wearing of gold, or of putting on of apparel; But let it be the hidden man of the heart, in that which is not corruptible, even the ornament of a meek and quiet spirit, which is in the sight of God of great price." (KJV)

Hidden in the above scripture is the Greek word *kruptos*, \ kroop·tos\, and it means "hidden, concealed, secret." True beauty that comes from within is often a mystery. There is a certain aura about a truly beautiful woman with inward beauty that cannot be attributed to her clothes, hair, jewelry, or make-up. It can't be laid to one thing; it is the total package of a woman that is beautiful. It is hidden inside her heart, and it shows up on the outside for others to see. This type of beauty cannot be bought with money. It comes from a genuine relationship with Christ. Inward beauty makes others wonder and say things like, "I can't put my finger on it, but that woman is beautiful." The Bible states in Colossians 1:27 that the mystery is "Christ in you, the hope of glory."

I don't believe that the Word of God is saying that women shouldn't braid their hair or wear jewelry or make-up, although some have interpreted it that way. You can be saved and still look sexy. The scripture means that you shouldn't order your universe around your hair, clothes, or make-up. True beauty is so much more than that. The outward appearance should not be what consumes one's thoughts and actions. A meek and quiet spirit is what a woman should adorn herself with whether she is wearing jewelry and make-up or not. A meek and quiet spirit is not about personality. Someone can be an extrovert and very strong willed and still put on a meek and quiet spirit. It's just like wearing braided hair, jewelry, and make-up; you have to adorn yourself or put it on. One can put on a meek and quiet spirit and watch true beauty radiate outwardly.

Now I know that this a challenge for some to even think about, so let's look a little deeper at what this means and how to do it. First of all, it has to be intentional. Because it is not about your personality, it may not come naturally. There has to be a concerted effort made to put on a meek and quiet spirit just like there is to put on jewelry and make-up because you don't always wear them. They must be applied. A meek and quiet spirit can be applied when one understands that meekness is not weakness. "Meek" in the above referenced scripture is translated from the Greek word *praus* \prah·ooce\, and it means "mildness of disposition, gentleness of spirit, meekness." The Greek word for quiet is *hesuchios* \hay·soo·khee·os\, and it essentially means "peaceable and tranquil." You don't have to be loud and abrasive to get your point across. You can be meek when you trust God because you know that God has your best interest at heart and that He will fight your battles.

There is a certain confidence and boldness that is at the heart of this type of meekness and quietness, and the beauty is in knowing that God has your back. Your meek and quiet spirit must overshadow anything else. It should be greater than any hairstyle, outfit, make-up, or jewelry that you may choose to wear. You may get attention through a glance at your body, clothes, shoes, or hair; but you must keep attention through the beauty hidden within your heart. You reap what you sow; and if you sow to the flesh, you will reap corruption as the Bible states (in Galatians 6:6). If you attract with flesh, you will reap a flesh conscious person. A woman must have more in her repertoire than seduction. Therefore, if you live by the saying that "beauty is only skin deep," you can find yourself knee deep in trouble!

The Bible states in I Timothy 2:9-10 "In like manner also, that women adorn, themselves in modest apparel, with shamefacedness and sobriety; not with braided hair, or gold, or pearls, or costly array; But (which becometh women professing godliness) with good works." Shamefacedness" in Greek is *aidos* \ ahee· doce\, and it means "a sense of shame or honour, modesty, bashfulness, reverence, regard for others, respect." Respect is what you must adorn yourself with. When you respect yourself, others will respect you. When a woman respects herself, she dresses modestly, not with everything hanging out for the world to see. A sense of bashfulness goes a long way. True beauty is shown in the way a woman carries herself whether she has her hair braided or weaved or whether she is wearing jewelry and make-up or not. She must carry herself with dignity, honor, and respect in order for her true beauty to be seen.

"Beauty is in the eye of the beholder."

I have heard stories of women who have breast cancer describing the experiences of losing their hair, going through chemotherapy, and losing their breasts. They have shared that it strips women of all the outward appearances of beauty and what it means to be a woman. They have also told of the power of coming to the realization that they are still beautiful women because of the love that they have in their hearts for their families and their inward strength to survive and live. Even with bald heads and no breasts, they have come to know and radiate true beauty from within, and others are able to see it! It is often said that "beauty is in the eye of the beholder." This simply means that the one looking at the object determines whether the thing is beautiful or not. Therefore, two people can look at the same thing and one can see beauty and the other can see ugliness.

There are some things that are said to be universally beautiful. Sunrises and sunsets, mountains and oceans, flowers, and other views of nature are a few things that we generally agree are breathtakingly beautiful. We often agree that most babies and some baby animals are beautiful. When it comes to people, there are varying opinions about beauty, and the saying "beauty is in the eye of the beholder" rings very true. We come to understand basically that beauty is subjective and that therefore it is based upon the viewer's perceptions, beliefs, and concepts of what beauty is. This is powerful because when we realize beauty is subjective we understand that we don't have to try and fit into a certain mold or type of beauty that is set by society. We can embrace our uniqueness and experience beauty on a whole different level when we aren't trying to be beautiful to everyone and everything.

Although you may not be beautiful to everyone you can rest assured that you are beautiful to God! As we walk in that revelation and really believe it, we will become beautiful to ourselves; and others will see our beauty as well. Oftentimes we cannot see the beauty that resides in us because of what others have said to us or about us as we were growing up. If you are told you are ugly, fat, or dark; have big teeth or are too skinny, etc., it can have a devastating effect on your self-image. Oftentimes, our first mirrors are our mothers, fathers, and other family members; and they can say less than flattering things about us and cause us to have self-concepts that are low indeed. I experienced that growing up. I was told things like, "Your butt is too big." Now, mind you, I have been blessed with a lot of "caboose" back there; however, as a developing young lady I only had a negative image concerning my bottom based upon what was said about me at home. It wasn't until later in life that I began to meet beholders who thought that part of my anatomy was very beautiful indeed.

What if I had been told, "You are beautiful, Rosalind," not "Your butt it too big," "You are too dark," or "Your hair is too nappy." During your formative years, those that are closest to you are your eyes. They mirror back to you what they see. If what they see and speak is negative, that negative image is seared into your subconscious until something happens in your life to remove it. When I look at pictures of myself as a young girl growing up, I am surprised to see how beautiful I actually was. I just wish I had been told sooner, so I could have seen myself the way I really am. It wasn't until I had a relationship with the Lord that I was able to see myself through His eyes. As He beheld my beauty, I felt beautiful; and I was able to see and believe that I am beautiful. The ultimate beholder is God Almighty! When He beholds us, we behold Him; and as we behold His beauty, we become what we behold; and that is *beautiful*!

Affirmation: "I Am Beautiful!"

You Are

You are the beat of my heart,
The blink of my eye,
The tears that I cry;
You are the air that I breathe,
The hope that I need,
The sweat that runs down my brow;
Sometimes I look around at all of the love and ask the question how?
Could someone love me so truly, the way that you do?
It makes me want to shout and run and tell all of the world
What a beautiful pearl you are!
You are the air that I breathe,
The love that I need,
The one that makes me whole;
You are the issues of life,
The essence of love,
The one that floods my soul;
I love you!
How could I ever repay day after day of bliss?
My only regret is this:
The time that was lost, and the moments that we missed;
I will love you throughout eternity!

CHAPTER 2

Beauty for Ashes

Unlocking Beauty from Within!

In the Book of Isaiah 61:3, it states, "To appoint unto them that mourn in Zion, to give unto them beauty for ashes, the oil of joy for mourning, the garment of praise for the spirit of heaviness; that they might be called trees of righteousness, the planting of the LORD, that he might be glorified. (KJV) The Hebrew word for beauty in the above scripture is *pâ'er* \peh·ayr\, and it means "a head-dress, ornament, turban." The Hebrew word for ashes is *'epher* \ay·fer\; it means "ashes," and figuratively it means "worthlessness." The Lord is making the declaration that He will give "beauty for ashes" to those who are mourning and feeling worthless because of the stains of the past or present circumstances.

Oftentimes, we have a tendency to feel bad and ugly because of things we may have done in our past. No matter how beautiful you may be, it can be overshadowed by the things that have happened to you. Sometimes, it is subconscious mourning where you are, grieving the loss of innocence and past hurts and shame. Mourning is usually accompanied by crying; and, ladies, you know what crying can do to your appearance. Crying can produce dark circles under swelled, red eyes; mascara and make-up smearing; red nose that is running; and inevitably, hair messed up and standing straight up on your head! Have you ever been there? I know I have many times before. It's hard to look beautiful while in mourning because of the "ashes" that you have been feeding on. Isaiah 44:20 states, "He feedeth on ashes: a deceived heart hath turned him aside, that he cannot deliver his soul, nor say, Is there not a lie in my right hand?" (KJV)

The worthlessness that you are feeling is really deception; and it can put you in a very downcast, ugly mood. The truth is found in the good news in Isaiah 61:3 because it is a prophesy talking about Jesus Christ. As a matter of fact it is within the context of this prophesy that we are given a glimpse of the things that Jesus was to accomplish through the anointing of the Holy Spirit when He came as the Messiah. Jesus Christ came to take away the worthlessness that represents the ashes of our lives and give us beauty.

The way He does it is revealed in the following few verses of Isaiah 61:3: they say that the Lord will give us, "beauty for ashes, the oil of joy for mourning and the garment of praise for the spirit of heaviness." The oil of joy is the anointing that we need in order to receive beauty for ashes. The word "joy" in this scripture literally means to rejoice and be glad. Whenever we decide to rejoice in the midst of mourning, it begins the process of beautification. Smiling is often associated with gladness. A smile does more for the face than a ton of make-up or jewelry ever could! Smiling that comes from a heart of joy exudes beauty. Studies show that smiling makes a person appear more intelligent and adds beauty and radiance, just as a downcast, frowning face can make the most beautiful person appear ugly.

Joy is the Holy Ghost make-up that we need to put on every day. I learned this principle a long time ago when I began to "watch my face." By that I mean I began to be conscious of my facial expressions, and I began to make a concerted effort to smile more and to smile with my eyes. I immediately began to get more compliments even from strangers, who would say to me, "You have a beautiful smile." That's all I needed to hear in order for me to adapt smiling as a part of my beauty regime. Now I smile often from a heart of joy.

There is healing power in laughter, which is a sign of joy. The Bible states in the Book of Proverbs 15:13, "A merry heart maketh a cheerful countenance: but by sorrow of the heart the spirit is broken." (KJV) In Proverbs 17:22, we read, "A merry heart doeth good like a medicine: but a broken spirit drieth the bones." (KJV) Sometimes when you are going through situations that are painful, such as the loss of a loved one to death, the loss of a relationship, the loss of a job, sickness, and other tragedies, you may not feel like smiling and rejoicing, much less laughing. The Bible states that "weeping may endure for a night but joy cometh in the morning" (Psalm 30:5) and "they that sow in tears shall reap in joy." (Psalm 126:5) These scriptures are powerful because they allow us to see that while sorrowful weeping will come, it is only meant to be temporary; and it is actually a seed that is sown to produce the fruit of joy. That is powerful!

I have found that in order for joy to come in the morning, you have to look for it. Joy is not dependent upon your circumstances; it is actually a by-product of a Spirit-filled life. Whenever you have access to the Holy Spirit, you always have access to joy because He is the carrier of joy. It is He that anoints us with the oil of joy. The anointing oil for our lives is the Holy Spirit, so when He is present in our lives through our personal relationship with Jesus, He is ready, willing, and able to fill our hearts with joy at any given time! Wow! We have the power to heal ourselves by allowing the Holy Spirit to flood our hearts with joy.

One way to access this joy and receive our beauty for ashes is found in the next part of Isaiah 61:3, which refers to "a garment of praise for the spirit of heaviness." When we praise God in spite of the circumstances, when we say, "Hallelujah anyhow," when we think of the goodness of Jesus and open up our mouths with the fruit of our lips giving thanks, that allows the Lord to change our countenance, our circumstances, and ultimately our

Rosalind Y. Tompkins

lives and make us into "those trees of righteousness" planted by the Lord for His glory.

Affirmations: **"Today I will smile!"**
"Today I will praise the Lord!"

I Am the Joy

When I look into the mirror, tell me, What do I see?
The reflection of the Glory, staring back at me!
The essence of Christ is who I see;
And I realize that it is no longer me, but we.
For <u>I am the Joy</u> that was set before my Lord,
As He hung, bled, and died on the cross-for my sins;
Creation cried and thought it was the end.
But today, I know that it didn't end, but begin.
For <u>I am the Joy!</u>
As I go throughout my day burdened by the weight of the world,
I stop and realize, as I look into His eyes, that <u>I am the Joy!</u>
I am the one that He saw and decided to stay on that cross so that I wouldn't be lost.
<u>I am the Joy</u> and because I am, I can laugh and not cry, smile and not frown, live and not die!
I can continue to try and try to reach the goal of my soul—being with my Savior.
Every day it carries me along the way, just to know that <u>I am the Joy!</u>

CHAPTER 3

Beautiful Feet

Unlocking Beauty from Within!

When we broach the subject of beauty, feet do not generally come to mind. We often think about the face, eyes, hair, or smile, when we say someone looks beautiful. Those are some of the first things that we consider in making a judgment as to the beauty of a person. Therefore, I was very surprised when I first read the scripture in Isaiah 52:7 that states, "How beautiful on the mountains are the feet of him that bring good news, who proclaim peace, who bring good tidings, who proclaim salvation, who say to Zion, "Your God reigns!" (NIV)

As a minister of the Gospel, I must admit that when I first read this scripture, I looked at my feet immediately to determine whether they were indeed beautiful. I didn't find them particularly attractive. It wasn't until years later that I received a revelation about this scripture. I began to realize that the beauty was in carrying the word of God. Those who carry the "good news" of the word of God are beautiful from head to feet, especially the feet, because it is the feet that bear the weight of the whole body. It is the feet that clock miles and miles each day, week, month, and year going about the business of living. When those feet are the feet of messengers of God, they automatically become beautiful because the message that they carry is beautiful. The message beautifies the messenger from head to feet!

The Hebrew word for beautiful in the referenced scripture is *na'ah* \naw·aw\, and it means "to be comely, be beautiful, be befitting". Another word for befitting is "appropriate"; and therefore I ask the question, How appropriate are your feet? In others words, are your feet appropriately attired to bring the "good news"? Have you ever thought about that? Whether you are a minister or not, your feet need to be appropriately attired. In the Bible days, there was no public transportation as we know it today. Everyone either walked or rode animals on unpaved, dusty roads. It required long and tiresome journeys just to get from point A to point B. Therefore, you had to have strong feet or have on the right shoes or sandals in order to endure the trip.

Today, metaphorically speaking, we still need to have strong feet and have on the right shoes to endure the trip. I am not talking about designer labels or stiletto pumps. I am talking about your walk with the Lord. Are your feet prepared to endure the many trials and tribulations, peaks and valleys, and unchartered territory that the Holy Spirit will lead you through? Your feet are symbolic of your walk with God. How beautiful are the feet that not only carry the word of God, but live the word of God! St. James 1:22-25 states, "But be ye doers of the word, and not hearers only, deceiving your own selves. For if any be a hearer of the word, and not a doer, he is like unto a man beholding his natural face in a glass: For he beholdeth himself, and goeth his way, and straightway forgetteth what manner of man he was. But whoso looketh into the perfect law of liberty, and continueth therein, he being not a forgetful hearer, but a doer of the work, this man shall be blessed in his deed." (KJV) Isn't it amazing how the writer of St. James uses the metaphor of looking into a mirror to explain the concept of being a doer and not a hearer of the word?

The point of the matter is you must continue in the word, and then the word of God becomes the mirror; and as you continue to behold the word, you become like the word. You become what you behold. So I ask the question, "What are you looking at?"

If you look into the mirror of the word of God long enough, you will become beautiful indeed all the way from your head to your feet!

It is very important to take care of your feet. Sometimes we get all clean and dressed up in our best, but neglect to take care of our feet. We need to do more than just put on a nice pair of shoes; we need to make sure our feet are properly taken care of. I have a friend who would be clean from head to ankles, but her feet would be ashy, bumpy, and downright ugly. One day I jestingly told her, "Girl, your feet are tore up from the floor up!" I asked her to please come with me to get a pedicure. About a year later, one day while we were riding in her car, I asked her to take me to a nail salon. I was totally shocked when she said, "I want to go in and get my feet done!" I was more than happy to have her come in with me. When we got to the nail salon, she was waited on immediately. Eventually I was seated beside her in a big black comfortable massaging chair. I placed my feet in the soothing hot bubble water and began to doze off. I was awakened by a sound coming from the seat next to mine. When I looked around, lo and behold, the nail technician was scraping the dead skin off of my friend's feet. She scraped and scraped and scraped; skin was flying everywhere, and the sweet nail technician just smiled and said, "You don't come here often, do you?" I looked at my friend, and she looked embarrassed with a painted-on smile. I laughed inside and closed my eyes again. On the ride home she said, "Wow, I didn't know my feet were supposed to be this color!" We both started laughing, and I told her to promise me she would go every two weeks!

No matter the size, width, or shape of our feet, we must not neglect them by wearing unsafe shoes that damage our feet just for the sake of looks. Shoes that are too small and too tight can ruin your whole attitude. If you have ever walked for blocks in high heeled shoes, you know exactly what I mean. I once participated in a field trip when I was a part of the Leadership Tallahassee program Class 24. This field trip involved walking to different buildings downtown for a scavenger hunt. I must tell you that by the end of the day, my "dogs were howling!"

Rosalind Y. Tompkins

I couldn't think straight; I wanted to get out of those shoes so badly. I thought about how women are encouraged to dress for success by wearing pumps that are stylish, but not comfortable at all. I see young ladies wearing high stilettos because some men think they are sexy; all the while, they are dancing, singing, talking, and walking in pain. This should not be so. We must take care of our feet and keep them beautiful and pampered, especially as we carry the "good news" of the Gospel. Remember two C's: cute and comfortable. I know if we can travel to the moon, we can create cute and comfortable shoes!

Affirmations: **"My feet are beautiful!"**
"I walk by faith and not by sight!"
"I am a doer of God's word!"

Destiny's Calling

Look through the door of infinity and see Destiny calling.
Smell the wind as it tickles your nose and blows open the door.
Walk into the place where time and space cease to be.
Destiny is waiting patiently.
Water falls and engulfs the air.
Cries of laughter are everywhere.
Singing and dancing; walking and prancing,
"Live life to fullest," Destiny saying.
"No time for worry, doubt, and fear,"
"It's time for love and living here."
Hours pass that seem like minutes floating on a cloud,
Time is spent and the sun is no more.
Hesitantly, I walk back through the door, of infinity.
I glance back as Destiny winks and blows a kiss;
With tears and a smile, I know I'll miss this place.
Destiny is calling, can't you hear?
    Walk into the place where time and space cease to be.
Destiny is waiting patiently!

CHAPTER 4

Ageless Beauty

Unlocking Beauty from Within!

Throughout the ages, man has searched for the "fountain of youth"—that magic water that would keep one young and beautiful forever. Of course, through much peril and disappointment, man has found that to be a myth. There is no potion that can keep you young and beautiful forever. There are, however, characteristics and qualities that you can acquire and adopt that will make and keep you beautiful, no matter what age you are. I would like to explore five: **Wonder, Kindness, Humor, Love, and Godliness.** Whenever you possess these characteristics and qualities, you are beautiful from the inside out; and it doesn't matter if you are one or one hundred and one, you are beautiful!

Wonder

According to *Merriam-Webster's Collegiate Dictionary,* Tenth Edition, "wonder" *(*noun*)* means "a cause of astonishment or admiration; the quality of exciting amazed admiration; rapt attention or astonishment at something awesomely mysterious or new to one's experience." Wonder is a quality that we see in babies and young children as they are growing and experiencing life outside the womb for the first time. I have a granddaughter, Tayla, who amazes me every day as I watch her grow and explore everything with wide eyes and a ready smile. She is so beautiful, not just in her physical attributes, but in her zest for life. She can go back to the same thing that fascinates her over and over again; she'll touch, feel, and ultimately attempt to eat the object of her interest. She was born with inherent wonder.

To a certain extent, some more than others, we all are. We are born with an instinct to explore and to learn, and everything is a wonder. As we grow older, our experiences teach us to become more and more closed to the world around us. We can sometimes get a cynical attitude that says, "Been there, done that, and bought the t-shirt." Even as disciples of Christ, we can become immune to the things of God. We get desensitized by Hollywood movies, and we look for the spectacular to equate with the supernatural, and it becomes harder and harder to be open to the everyday wonders of God. Wonder is however a quality that we should never lose no matter what age. Wonder looks beautiful when it is genuine. When you are genuinely surprised and amazed with the freshness of life in the Holy Spirit, it causes your eyes to sparkle; and it produces a childlike expression that is beautiful indeed!

We can get a glimpse at the type of wonder that I am speaking of from an account of scripture that we find in the third chapter of Acts. There we are told the story of the man that was lame from birth and who lay at the gate called Beautiful begging for alms. Peter and John came by on their way to prayer when the man asked them for money. They did not give him money, but Jesus instead; and the man was instantly healed. (Acts 3:1-8) Once the former lame man began to leap and praise God, we see the results in Acts 3:9-11: "And all the people saw him walking and praising God: And they knew that it was he which sat for alms at the Beautiful gate of the temple: and they were filled with **wonder** and amazement at that which had happened unto him. And as the lame man which was healed held Peter and John, all the people ran together unto them in the porch that is called Solomon's, greatly **wondering**." The people were filled with wonder because they had seen the man lying at the Beautiful gate for years and now here he was standing, leaping, and praising God!

The Greek word for wonder in the referenced scripture is *thambos* \tham·bos\, and it means "to render immovable, amazement." The word used for wondering is another Greek word, *ekthambos* \ek·tham·bos\; and it means "quite astonished, amazed, terrifying, dreadful, to wonder or marvel greatly." When is the last time that you were rendered immovable or marveled greatly because of something that you experienced? Many of you may say, "Well, I haven't seen anything like that before." Not so fast; every day is filled with wonder. Just to wake up in the morning and have the activity of your limbs and to be clothed in your right mind is a wonder because everyone does not experience that. In other words, when we realize that living is a wonder and loving is a wonder, and God's blessing is a wonder, and breathing is a wonder, then we will began to have an open spirit willing and ready to experience greater wonders that are produced by our faith in the Lord Jesus Christ. It amazes me that the gate was called Beautiful because even though I know it was named that because it was a beautiful edifice, the wonder of God's miraculous healing makes everything and everyone Beautiful!

Affirmation: **"Today I am filled with Wonder!"**

Kindness

My mother always told us, "It doesn't cost you anything to be kind, but it costs you everything not to be!" That is a true saying because so many times we are faced with situations where we can be kind or as some would say, be "real." In other words, there are those who think that just because they are telling the truth, it's okay to be mean. For example, suppose someone asks you, "Do you like my hair?" If you really don't, you could say, "No," which is an honest answer, or, "Not really, but you are gorgeous anyway." Which response would make the other person feel good? The second one perhaps, but either answer is okay.

The problem is that many times when asked a subjective question like that, some people use it as an opportunity to be downright mean. They may say something like, "No, I don't like your hair; it looks like you stuck your finger in an electrical outlet, and your outfit stinks too; as a matter of fact, you always look like that." I have seen it happen time and time again; and when asked why they would say that, they say something to the effect of, "I was just telling the truth, and they asked me." These people actually think it is okay to say anything out of their mouths no matter the resulting consequence. This behavior can make the most attractive person ugly!

The opposite is true as well. Kindness is a beautiful quality that looks good on anyone. When you look into kind eyes and a kind expression, especially when you are in need of some type of assistance or if you have had a rough day, it really makes the person wearing kindness look very beautiful. Kindness is essentially having a sympathetic or helpful nature and being affectionate, loving, forbearing, and gentle. You can tell the truth and still be kind. It is not what you say, but the words you choose to use to say it and therefore how you say it. The Bible states that our words should be "seasoned with salt and full of grace" (Colossians 4:6). Ultimately, kindness is seen by our actions. It's not just words. It is doing good things for others when we have the opportunity. It is going that extra mile and not complaining. To be kind is to be beautiful no matter how old you are.

Colossians 3:12 states: "Put on therefore, as the elect of God, holy and beloved, bowels of mercies, **kindness**, humbleness of mind, meekness, longsuffering"; this scripture helps us to realize that kindness is something that we have to put on. It is not just going to come naturally all the time. There are times when you might not feel like being kind, but through the Holy Spirit you can be kind because that is also one of the fruit (In the bible it is singular) of the Spirit of God. Kindness is so attractive that children are drawn to kind people no matter how they look. Kindness looks good on toddlers, on senior citizens, and on everyone in between.

Affirmation: **"I am Kind!"**

Humor

The most important thing that one can do in order to remain beautiful is to laugh. I was talking with a friend who was going through a tremendous trial; and she said that she had gone to a gala event that featured a comedian for entertainment and that for thirty minutes they laughed and laughed. She stated that while she was there, she forgot all about the trials she was going through; and she felt happy and beautiful inside and out. She said that even though she was dressed up from head to toe, hair, shoes, purse, earrings, make-up, all synchronized; she didn't feel particularly attractive until she started laughing and was able to see her situation in a different light. A good sense of humor will make up for bad hair days, pimples, and bloating, that is, if you don't take yourself too seriously.

When you don't look or feel your best, look for the humor in your situation. Sometimes, just looking in the mirror and seeing how silly you look will cause you to laugh at yourself! Oftentimes, when women are asked for the qualities that they would like in a mate, they inevitably will say that they want someone who will make them laugh. Many comedians have testimonies of how they were popular in school because they made others laugh. Therefore, they were invited to all of the parties and events because they made others feel good.

Laughter can even the playing field, so to speak. If you feel that you are not exactly where you would like to be in the looks department, make up for the deficit with a good sense of humor and the ability to make others laugh. That will give you a beautiful quality that will carry you a long way, no matter what your looks may be.

"Humor," according to *Webster's Dictionary* means "the quality of inciting laughter, or of perceiving what is comical." It is good to be able to laugh and create laughter in others. That is a beautiful quality, especially in today's world, with so much bad news and so many depressing things going on. In order to have humor, you must look for it. Look for the absurd in everyday life and laugh. Point it out to others, so they can laugh as well. Be able to laugh at yourself, but don't make a practice of laughing at others. Laugh with others. There is the saying "Laugh and the whole world will laugh with you." Have you ever thought about how laughing is contagious? If you hear someone else laughing, it can trigger laughter in you. I have been in church services where all we did was laugh. There was Holy laughter that spread like a wild fire, and the whole congregation laughed for hours on end. It was so refreshing and beautiful. After those services, I felt as though I had been cleansed by the laughter.

Did you know that the Bible says that God sits in the heavens and laughs at those who take counsel together against the Lord and His anointed? (Psalm 2:1-4) I believe if God can laugh, then so can we. We can laugh at the devil and those who try to come up against us, because we know that in Christ we have the victory! Not only does God laugh at His enemies, it is clear throughout scripture that God has an awesome sense of humor. One account that comes to mind is the time when God came to Abraham and Sarah and told them that they would conceive a child in their old age—Abraham was one hundred years old, and Sarah was ninety. As a matter of fact, when Sarah overheard the conversation, she laughed, as did Abraham when the Lord first told him. I don't know about you, but I probably would have laughed as well! Ladies, can you imagine that? Even though women are conceiving at much older ages these days, ninety years old is a bit much! Well, of course, God had the last laugh; and when the promised child came, they even named him Isaac, which is the Hebrew word *Yitschaq* \yits·khawk\, and it means, "He laughs."

God has given us promises that are found in His word that are based upon our covenant with Him through the Lord Jesus Christ. Just as Sarah and Abraham laughed at the absurdity of the promise of a child given to them in their old age, we sometimes laugh and wonder if the promises that God makes to us will ever come to pass. Well, I want to ask you just as God asked Sarah, "Is anything too hard for the Lord?" (Genesis 18:14) The answer is a resounding, No! There is nothing too hard for God; therefore, go ahead and laugh in advance because it is surely coming to pass. Everything that God has promised to you is coming to pass!

I made up in my mind a long time ago that I would laugh as much as possible. I also realized that I had a gift to make others laugh. I am not talking about obscenity, foolish talk, or coarse joking, which according to the Bible is out of place (Ephesians 5:4). But I am talking about making light of serious issues or at least presenting them in such a way as to help others see the absurdity in life and laugh with me. I have found that medicine goes down much better with laughter. My daughter calls me silly, and I know exactly what she means. I allow myself to think of things that will make me laugh and to say things that will make others laugh usually in a playful, lighthearted way. I never laugh at others at their expense or try to put others down to get a laugh. When I laugh, I want God to laugh with me and through me.

Affirmation: **"Today I will laugh!"**

Love

The true essence of love is beautiful. The one who loves and the object of the one loving are both made beautiful by love. The Bible states that God is love (I John 4:8). The Greek word used for love in the referenced scripture is *agape* \ag·ah·pay\, and it means "brotherly love, affection, good will, love, benevolence." It is the God kind of love that is unconditional. It is not dependent upon the one being loved, but it is dependent upon the one loving. The scripture (John 3:16) states, "For God so loved the world, that he gave his only begotten son, that whosoever believeth in him should not perish, but have everlasting life." (KJV) We realize that it wasn't about the world so much as it was about God. God's love is what caused Him to give His only begotten son, Jesus, not the world.

When you love as God loves, you realize that the love is coming forth from you, not based upon what the other person does or doesn't do; but it is based upon the love that is on the inside of you. You cannot fall out of unconditional love because you don't fall into it. You make a choice to love and a choice to continue loving. That's the beauty of love. That is why there is no greater force than love.

I have been in and out of love on many occasions throughout my lifetime, and I have come to the conclusion that the greatest love is the love of God. God's love is a love that surrounds you and keeps you no matter what is going on in your life. The Bible says that "the Lord will never leave you nor forsake you," and I have found that to be true. (Hebrews 13:5) So many times when the going gets tough, the tough get going, but not God. I have found that when the going gets tough, the Lord sticks even closer. In the good times and in the bad times, He is always there. When I am up and when I am down or when I am right and when I am wrong, the Lord is always there to help me make it through. That is love and that is beautiful!

The Bible states in John 15:13, "Greater love hath no man than this, that a man lay down his life for his friends. (KJV) True love involves sacrifice. You must be willing to give up your life for the ones that you love. Oftentimes, this type of love can be found in the family constellation where mothers and fathers give up their very lives for the sake of their children. I have heard of hundreds of testimonies where mothers have given up so much just to make sure that their children had a good life. That is what I did as a single parent. I gave up the world and all of the things that I had been into that were contrary to the will of God when I had my daughter, Janar. I worked and made sure she was adequately taken care of, and I did it all with joy because of my love for her. That is exactly what Abba Father did when He sent Jesus Christ into this world. And that is precisely what Jesus did when He sacrificed His life by dying on the cross for those who would believe in Him in order to have eternal life. Jesus became the ultimate sacrifice of the lamb slain from the foundation of the world (Revelation 13:8). That is our example. If we say we love, we must be willing to give up everything in order for the ones that we love to be safe and secure.

The New Testament is a covenant of love. As a matter of fact, the Bible states in the Book of Matthew 22:37-40, "Jesus said unto him, Thou shalt love the Lord thy God with all thy heart, and with all thy soul, and with all thy mind. This is the first and great commandment. And the second is like unto it, Thou shalt love thy neighbour as thyself. On these two commandments hang all the law and the prophets." (KJV) These particular scriptures outline for us the order of love.

Yes, there is an order to love, and so many times we fail in our love relationships because we are out of order. The order is number one: love God with all your heart, soul, and mind. This requires putting and keeping God first and foremost before anything and anyone. Number two: love your neighbor. Number three: as you love yourself. So we see that we must love our neighbor as we love ourselves, and that mandates that we follow the golden rule, which is, Do unto others as you would have others to do unto you. In other words, love is an action word; and when we love, we show forth that love through our actions.

So many times we cannot love others appropriately because we do not love ourselves; and we do not love ourselves because we do not love God and because, as we see in the scripture referenced above, "God is love." When we put love in the right order, we get the right results; and that is beautiful. We love God, others, and then ourselves. So many times, we love selfishly. We are so concerned about, "What's in it for me?" until we cannot think of anyone but ourselves. We love ourselves; then we love God and others. Or sometimes we do not love ourselves, but we attempt to love others and put them before God. Any combination of love other than the order that God establishes will produce a skewed or perverted type of love. We must love God with total abandonment, and that includes keeping His commandments. When God is placed in the proper order, we love ourselves because we truly know that we are made in the image of God. It is within that context that we can truly love others.

Affirmations: **"God loves me!"**
                "I love God!"
                "I love others!"
                "I love myself!"

Godliness

To be godly essentially means to be and act like God. We can look all around at God's creation and see beauty. We can look at one another and see beauty exuding from the eyes and hearts of our fellowmen. The Bible states that "We are created in the image of God" (Genesis 1:26-27). Therefore, if the image is beautiful, then we know that the genuine article, God, is exceedingly beautiful; and so, to be godly is to be beautiful. God is holy, and we as believers in Christ are admonished to be holy, as He is holy (I Peter 1:16); for without holiness, no one shall see God (Hebrews 12:14). To be godly is to be holy.

"Holiness" in the referenced scripture is the Greek word, *hagiasmos* \hag·ee·as·mos\. It is also translated as "sanctification"; and it means "consecration, purification, the effect of consecration, and sanctification of heart and life." The Bible states in Psalm 96:9, "O worship the LORD in the beauty of holiness: fear before him, all the earth." Holiness means to be set apart unto God in this particular scripture. Some people believe that to be holy is to be drab and unattractive, but the opposite is true. To live a life that is set apart for the Master's use is beautiful! We are to live a life of worship and holiness unto the Lord so that His beauty will shine through us.

The Bible states that "godliness with contentment is great gain" (I Timothy 6:6). In this particular scripture, the Greek word for "godliness" is *eusebeia* \yoo·seb·i·ah\, and it means "reverence, respect, piety towards God, godliness." So many times we want to look a certain way in order to attract people; but it is not all in how we look, but also in how we are. Whenever you are living a godly and holy life that is set apart from the world and unto God, then you should be content to know that you are beautiful in the sight of God and others who know the Lord. There is so much godlessness that is perpetuated in our society among young and old alike, until the quality of godliness is almost an extinct concept. Living godly is such a commodity these days, until it automatically causes one to stand out and be noticed. It produces a sweet beauty that is unparalleled, compared with any of the vulgar and filthy images of beauty that are masquerading for the real thing.

One might ask the question, "How can I obtain this quality of godliness?" The answer is found in the word of God. The Bible states in 2 Peter 1:3, "According as his divine power hath given unto us all things that pertain unto life and **godliness**, through the knowledge of him that hath called us to glory and virtue" (KJV). We receive godliness through our knowledge of Jesus Christ. Once we spend time in the word of God and grasp an understanding of what it means to be a disciple of Christ, our minds can be renewed to the things and ways of the Lord. As the Bible states, "old things are passed away and all things are become new (II Corinthians 5:17). This process is ongoing and it is not going to happen overnight. As a matter of fact, it will happen over a life time so relax and enjoy the journey in godliness.

Affirmations: "I am created in the image of God!"
"I am Godly!"

Remember, whenever you possess the characteristics and qualities of **Wonder, Kindness, Humor, Love, and Godliness,** you are beautiful from the inside out; and it doesn't matter if you are one or one hundred and one—you are beautiful!

Rosalind Y. Tompkins

I Remember

Memories flood my heart with images of times gone by.
It makes me want to cry to feel the reasons why
Life seems to pass me by.
Memories of days of rest while lying on your chest, melting in your arms far away from harm's way.
The warmth of your touch, the love in your eyes, the feeling of surprise as grace melts with sin, helping me to begin again and again.
Memories flood my mind thinking of a time when hope was at the door, begging me for more of what life has to offer.
Thank you for the memories of times past and times to be;
The memories make me free to believe in possibilities; they bring me to my knees, anticipating, waiting, listening, and remembering you!

CHAPTER 5

Sex Is Beautiful

Unlocking Beauty from Within!

Sex is God's idea. He created us and gave us the ability to procreate through the act of sexual intercourse. He also made us with the ability to experience pleasure in the process. It is a shame before God how humanity has perverted and made ugly such a beautiful and sacred union.

In the Book of Genesis 4:1 it states, "And Adam **knew** Eve his wife; and she conceived, and bare Cain, and said, I have gotten a man from the LORD." (KJV) This is the first time that we are introduced to procreation through husband and wife sexual intercourse in the word of God. Before that, God created everything just by speaking it into existence until he formed man from the dust and Eve from Adam's rib.

The scripture uses the word "knew" to describe the act. In this particular scripture, knew is the Hebrew word *yada'* \ yaw·dah\; and it means "to know, learn to know, to perceive, and see, find out and discern, discriminate, distinguish, know by experience, recognize, admit, acknowledge, confess, to consider, to be acquainted with." In the New Testament, in Matthew 1:25, sexual intercourse is also described by the word "knew." In Greek, the word is *ginosko* \ghin·oce·ko\; and it means the same thing as the Hebrew word *yada*; but the definition also states that it is a "Jewish idiom for sexual intercourse between a man and a woman." I believe that it is very significant that the Bible uses the word "knew" to describe the act of sexual intercourse, because that is precisely what is supposed to happen within the context of the sexual relationship between husbands and wives as depicted in the Bible. There is to be a knowing of the other person, not just physically in a sexual way, but intimately, the way you would know someone deep inside as a soul mate.

The problem in our society is that people are having sex with people they don't even know casually much less intimately. There is no true union of the heart, spirit, and soul that comes with knowing the other person. There is no marriage covenant that is made in the sight of God and man. There is just an animalistic lust, which results in sexual encounters that produce teenage pregnancy, single parent families, and broken hearts. And that is just the tip of the iceberg! When you add sexual abuse that takes place in too many families throughout the world, prostitution, pornography, and other perversions, then you see that sex has become downright ugly in many cases.

We have forgotten who we are created to be in the sight of God; and even among Christians, there is rampant sex outside of marriage and adultery within marriage. This should not be so! The Bible states in I Corinthians 6:12-20, "All things are lawful unto me, but all things are not expedient: all things are lawful for me, but I will not be brought under the power of any. Meats for the belly, and the belly for meats: but God shall destroy both it and them. Now the body is not for **fornication**, but for the Lord; and the Lord for the body. And God hath both raised up the Lord, and will also raise up us by his own power. Know ye not that your bodies are the members of Christ? shall I then take the members of Christ, and make them the members of an harlot. God forbid. What? know ye not that he which is joined to an harlot? is one body? for two, saith he, shall be one flesh. But he that is joined unto the Lord is one spirit. Flee **fornication**. Every sin that a man doeth is without the body; but he that committeth fornication sinneth against his own body. What? know ye not that your body is the temple of the Holy Ghost which is in you, which ye have of God, and ye are not your own? For ye are bought with a price: therefore glorify God in your body, and in your spirit, which are God's. (KJV) In the scriptures referenced above, the Greek word for fornication is *porneia* \por·ni·ah\; and it means "illicit sexual intercourse, adultery, fornication, homosexuality, lesbianism, intercourse."

We must flee fornication and run into God. The above scripture states that whenever we are joined unto the Lord, we are one spirit and our bodies belong to God; therefore, we are to honor God in what we do with our bodies. So many times single women ask the question, "What am I supposed to do with myself if I am not married?" The answer is found in the word of God. The Bible states in Romans 12:1 that we are to "present our bodies to the Lord as a living sacrifice." To present our bodies to the Lord is a sacrifice because that means we are not participating in fornication of any kind, and that is a sacrifice.

But the scripture also says that it is our "reasonable service." It is what we are supposed to do as Disciples of Christ. When we flee fornication and run into the Lord, we are given power to resist the temptations of the flesh. The Bible says if we walk in the Spirit we will not fulfill the lust of the flesh (Galatians 5:16). To walk in the Spirit means to spend time in prayer, in the word of God, and in communion and fellowship with the Lord Jesus Christ through the precious Holy Spirit. In the New Testament the Greek word for "communion" is *koinonia* \koy·nohn·ee·ah\; and it means "fellowship, association, community, communion, joint participation, intercourse, the share which one has in anything, intimacy." The Lord wants us to be intimate with Him, not in a fleshly way but by the Spirit. When you develop an intimate relationship with the Lord, He will keep you if you want to be kept. He will fill your heart, soul, and body with the goodness of the Lord; He will give you peace that passes all understanding; He will give you hope and a future; He will give you joy like a river and full of glory.

The Bible states in Psalm 16:11, Thou "wilt shew me the path of life: in thy presence is fulness of joy; at thy right hand there are **pleasures** for evermore (KJV). In the referenced scripture the Hebrew word for "pleasure" is *na'iym*\naw·eem\; and it means "pleasant, delightful, sweet, lovely, agreeable, beautiful (physical)." I have found this to be true in my life. It is indeed pleasant, delightful, sweet, lovely, and beautiful to be in the presence of God! We access this pleasure from the Lord primarily through prayer and worship. A heart that worships the Lord in Spirit and in truth is a heart that communes with the Lord. Once you enter into the place of fellowship with God, then you move out of the realm of the flesh; and you will no longer participate in the sins of the flesh, and that is beautiful! You don't have to worry about catching a sexually transmitted disease or having an unplanned pregnancy. You will have assurance that God will provide for you; and if and when the time comes for you to be united in holy matrimony with your spouse, you will be ready; and the union will be beautiful and undefiled.

Some people may say, "That is all well and good, but I need someone that I can touch and that will hold me close." That is what the flesh desires; but in actuality what you need is the Lord, and He will provide everything else in His timing, including that person who will hold you close. The Bible states in Ecclesiastes 3:11, "He hath made every thing **beautiful** in his time: also he hath set the world in their heart, so that no man can find out the work that God maketh from the beginning to the end." Don't worry, God is going to make you and your situation beautiful—just trust and wait on Him!

Affirmations: **"My body belongs to God!"**
"I will glorify God with my body!"
"I will glorify God with my spirit!
"My body is a temple of God!"
"The Holy Spirit lives in me!"
"God makes everything beautiful in His time!"

Marriage

- It's like honeybees and blueberries with the sun shining bright in the night.
- It's like summertime and nursery rhymes with the sun shining bright in the day.
- It's like feelings lost and found on a merry-go-round spinning out of control.
- Nobody told me that it would be like rain in the night, with your heart squeezed tight, singing songs of rejoicing and praise.
- Lollypops and spinning tops, roses with thorns and cactuses with horns, living and loving where two becomes one.
- Oh what fun, parades in the street, dancing to the beat of your heart as it plays in my head.
- Nobody said that it would be the last and the first, the best and the worst, the ultimate thirst, fulfilled!
- It's like strawberries and bumblebees with Christ shining bright in the day and the night.
- It's like loving hard, while thanking God for the one created to walk with you.
- Through the thick and the thin, until the very end of life as we know it right now!

CHAPTER 6

Clothed in Beauty

Unlocking Beauty from Within!

In Genesis 2:25, the Bible states about Adam and Eve, "And they were both **naked**, the man and his wife, and were not ashamed." It is amazing how they did not realize they did not have any clothes on until after the fall. After they ate from the tree of good and evil, the first thing that happened was that they saw that they were naked, "And the eyes of them both were opened, and they knew that they were naked; and they sewed fig leaves together, and made themselves aprons" (Genesis 3:7 KJV). The Hebrew word for "knew" in the referenced scripture is *yada'* \yaw·dah\ (See Chapter 5, "Sex Is Beautiful"). It denotes an intimate knowing of the other person.

Once they saw themselves in an intimate way, they realized they needed to cover up, and they made clothes out of leaves. The first thing that Adam talked to God about when he was caught hiding in the garden after the fall was his nakedness, "And he said, I heard thy voice in the garden, and I was afraid, because I was **naked**; and I hid myself (Genesis 3:10 KJV). The first question God asked Adam after the fall had to do with his nakedness, "And he said, Who told thee that thou wast **naked**? Hast thou eaten of the tree, whereof I commanded thee that thou shouldest not eat?" (Genesis 3:11 KJV) We see that this nakedness was a pretty big thing because all of a sudden Adam and Eve were self-conscious and not God-conscious.

Now Adam was hiding and afraid, not because he had eaten the forbidden fruit, but because he was naked; and he knew his nakedness was evidence of what he had done. The Lord knew they were naked all the time; but He knew someone had to tell Adam and Eve because they didn't realize they were naked before, and therefore they were not ashamed. The shame came when they saw their nakedness for the first time. How did that happen? Well, I believe when they ate from the tree not only were their eyes opened, but they also lost the covering of glory that clothed them before the fall. God had to make them clothes after He pronounced the consequence of their disobedience, "Unto Adam also and to his wife did the LORD God make coats of skins, and clothed them (Genesis 3:21KJV). Did the Lord neglect Adam and Eve and leave them naked and defenseless in the Garden when He first created them and then after the fall decide to clothe them? Of course not—before the fall they were clothed in God's, not animal, skin, and that was all they needed.

God's skin is His Glory! When Moses asked the Lord to "show me your glory" (Exodus 33:18 KJV), the Lord showed him parts of His body (Exodus 33:22-23). We know that what covers our body is skin. And since we are created in God's image, what covers God's body is His skin; and that happens to be His glory, and God's glory is beautiful!

Under the New Covenant, through the shed blood of our Lord and Savior Jesus Christ, God is again clothing His children with glory. The difference this time is the fact that He is clothing us from within and not from without. In other words, the glory is not just upon us, but it is actually in us! The Bible states in Colossians 1:26-27, "Even the mystery which hath been hid from ages and from generations, but now is made manifest to his saints: To whom God would make known what is the riches of the glory of this mystery among the Gentiles; which is Christ in you, the hope of glory."

In the above referenced scripture, the Greek word for "glory" is *doxa* \dox·ah\; and it means "splendor, brightness, magnificence, excellence, preeminence, dignity, grace, majesty." God's splendor, brightness, magnificence, excellence, majesty, resides in you as a child of God; and that is the true beauty that will cause one to shine brighter than the stars on a dark night.

God wants to clothe all of His creation in His glory. You might ask, "How in the world can I be clothed in God's glory?" Well, I am glad you asked. We can find the answer in the word of God. The Bible states, in 2 Corinthians 3:18, "But we all, with open face beholding as in a glass the **glory** of the Lord, are changed into the same image from **glory** to **glory**, even as by the Spirit of the Lord" (KJV). Changed in this particular scripture is the Greek word, *metamorphoo* \met·am·or·fo·o\, which means "to change into another form, to transform, to transfigure." Christ's appearance was changed and was resplendent with divine brightness on the mount of transfiguration. We are clothed in God's glory as we behold God's glory because we become what we behold.

Through the word of God, we are changed or transformed by the renewing of our minds into the image of our Lord and Savior, Jesus Christ. This work is done by the Holy Spirit. We move from one level of glory to another level of glory, and that becomes what we wear—God's glory. It's not so much about what you have on; it's about who you have inside of you. We all want to look nice and dress for success; however, it doesn't really matter if you are wearing designer clothes or designer knock-offs; you need to make sure you are clothed in God's glory. I have heard so many testimonies; and I can personally attest to being complimented and called beautiful by perfect strangers, not because of what I had on or how my hair was fixed, but simply because they were able to behold the glory of God radiating from within. There is a brightness that resides upon a person that is clothed in God's glory, an inner glow that shines brightly through the eyes of one who is filled with God's Spirit.

The Bible states in Luke 11:34, "The light of the body is the eye: therefore when thine eye is **single**, thy whole body also is full of light; but when thine eye is evil, thy body also is full of darkness (KJV). The Greek word for "single" is *haplous* hap·looce\; and it means "simple, single, whole, good fulfilling its office, sound, of the eye." Beauty is seen with the eyes and in the eyes. Eyes are windows to the heart and soul of a person; therefore, it is important that your eyes are single, whole, and sound so that they may reflect the light of God's glory. Singleness of eyes is obtained by keeping our eyes "fixed on Jesus the author and perfecter of our faith" (Hebrews 12:2. NIV). Let God clothe you with His glory today and everyday!

Affirmations: **"I am clothed with God's glory!"**
"I am filled with God's spirit!"

Greatness

Is this not the place where greatness begins?
Is this not the place where greatness ends?
Yes, this is the place where greatness begins, and this is the place where greatness ends.
In His presence the connection is made that lights the temple and lets up the shade; but this is also the place where the Glory of God outshines every other light.
Yes, this is the place where greatness begins, and this is the place where greatness ends—in His presence.

CHAPTER 7

Beautiful Wounds

Unlocking Beauty from Within!

A "wound," according to *Merriam-Webster's Collegiate Dictionary*, Tenth Edition, is "an injury to the body (as from violence, accident, or surgery) that involves laceration or breaking of a membrane (as the skin) and usually damage to underlying tissues; a mental or emotional hurt or blow."

I had surgery that left a bikini-cut scar at the base of my stomach. A couple of weeks after my surgery, I asked a close friend if she wanted to see my wound. She said, "No"; and I asked her why not, and she said, "I just don't." About a week later she came to my house and I asked her again jokingly if she wanted to see the place where I was cut open; initially, she again declined, and I said, "That's okay; I'll find someone who will." Before she left for home, she asked me to show it to her; and when I did, she said, "Wow, that looks good; God sure gave the doctors a gift to be able to sew you back together like that and for the wound to look that good so soon." I said, "Yes, that's because it is healing." She said "I thought it would look bloody and everything." I said to her, "Why would I want to show you that? I just wanted you to see the beauty of God's healing."

The reason I wanted my friend to see my wound is that I believe if you just see my beauty and not my scars, then you have not really seen me because my wounds are a part of my beauty. So many times it is our wounds and scars that we hide from the world and even from our family and closest friends. We mistakenly believe that if they see the scars, then they won't love us anymore. Well, if you have someone in your life that cannot look upon your scars and imperfections and still think you are beautiful and love you, then you don't need them in your life.

Some people will say, "I just don't like looking at ugly things like that." That is well and good; however, we all have wounds and scars. Some are visible, and some are invisible; but they are there nonetheless. Some scars are on the body, while others are on the heart; but both types are real and need to be shown and not hidden and covered up. They first must be shown and revealed to God, in order for the healing process to begin. God has seen everything and knows everything already. He has seen us at our worst and at our best, and He still loves us dearly. But we must not hide our wounds by not talking to God about them and pretending as if they don't exist.

God understands because He has scars of His own. The Bible says in Isaiah 53:5, in a prophecy about Jesus, "But he was **wounded** for our transgressions, he was bruised for our iniquities: the chastisement of our peace was upon him; and with his stripes we are healed (KJV). The prophecy was fulfilled when Jesus came and established the New Testament through His crucifixion, death, burial, and resurrection; and in 1Peter 2:24, it states, "Who his own self bare our sins in his own body on the tree, that we, being dead to sins, should live unto righteousness: by whose **stripes** ye were healed (KJV). The Greek word for "stripes," in this New Testament scripture is *molops* \mo·lopes\; and it means "a bruise, wale, wound that trickles with blood." There is healing power in the "stripes" and blood of Jesus!

When Jesus appeared to His disciples before ascending to heaven, He showed them the nail prints in His hands and the wounds in His side (John 20:27). The scars were evidence of what He had experienced. He used them to convince and rebuke His disciple Thomas (John 20:28-29). Jesus could have removed all signs of His crucifixion, but He chose not to do so. I know that His scars could not have been pretty given the excruciatingly painful death that He went through. However, it was important to keep them; and because of what they represent—salvation, healing, deliverance, and eternal life—they are beautiful. Your scars, too, are beautiful, precisely for the same reason. They represent a part of your life that you experienced and that by the grace of God, you survived! They are a reminder of God's goodness to you.

Many times, as mothers, we experience stretch marks during pregnancy that linger on after the birth of our children. I have heard young mothers talk about how they feel ugly because of their stretch marks. I always tell them not to focus on how the stretch marks look, but on what they represent. They are the battle scars of a mother, and the fathers of their children should love and appreciate every one of them! Pimples are another source of great dismay among many people. They come; and when they go, they sometimes leave marks. It's amazing how a woman can be stunningly beautiful in spite of the pimples, but still focus on them and feel ugly or compare herself to others who don't have pimples. We must reframe our thought process when it comes to wounds and scars. If you cannot remove them, then you might as well embrace them and call them beautiful because they are a part of you; and you are beautiful!

Affirmations: **"I will share my wounds with God!"**
"I will share my wounds with others!"
"My wounds represent my experiences!"
"My wounds are beautiful!"

Rosalind Y. Tompkins

Destiny Fulfilled

The time has come and the time is now.
You have been looking and searching because you didn't know how you were going to make it; you just couldn't take it.
The trials and tribulations of life got you down.
It got so bad until you thought you would drown in your own blood; but like a flood, the Spirit lifted up a standard and brought you through it.
Although you couldn't see it you made it to it—
the place of Destiny. You heard the call and had to Dream Again after the fall, because, after all, you believed inside that you are more than your problems, and more than your pain. You are much more than that; but all the same,
you had to know and do the Father's will because that is the way that Destiny is fulfilled!
Who you are is who you shall be; your purpose in life lies within.
Deep inside, you see you can win because greatness is there; and that is who you are.
When you trust in JESUS, then you can go far, high above the clouds and sit upon a star, and look down over your problems and say, Peace be Still,
because from where I'm sitting, Destiny is Fulfilled!

CHAPTER 8

Uniquely Beautiful

Unlocking Beauty from Within!

The Bible states, in 2 Corinthians 10:12, "For we dare not make ourselves of the number, or **compare** ourselves with some that commend themselves: but they measuring themselves by themselves, and **comparing** themselves among themselves, are not wise" (KJV). Comparison is one of the biggest problems that we have as it relates to our perception of beauty. We are given images of the supposedly ideal beauty through the media, as well as through the opinions of family and friends. Then we are left to compare ourselves to what has been lifted up as a model of beauty. The problem is that the ideal is often unattainable. Most of the pictures of the models that we see in the magazines are doctored and air-brushed to make the models look flawless. In addition to that, you have increasing numbers of women and men, who are getting cosmetic surgery to tuck, lift, pull, suck, and add to their bodies. Now tell me, what average person can compete with the images that are created by man to be the standard for beauty? The answer is slim to none, not many at all! Then why are the movies that portray women as anorexic beauty queens our guides? So many women feel bad about themselves after looking at magazines, television, and movies. They nearly starve themselves to death trying to lose weight; and if they have the money, they go and get unnecessary cosmetic surgery to add to their lips, hips, and breasts and take away from their thighs and bellies—all because they are comparing themselves to others; and as the scripture points out, this is not wise.

In Chapter 1, "What is Beauty?" I quoted Psalm 139:14: "I will praise thee; for I am fearfully and **wonderfully** made: marvellous are thy works; and that my soul knoweth right well (KJV); and I pointed out that the Hebrew word for "wonderfully" is *palah* \paw·law," which means "to be distinct, marked out, separated, distinguished." Wisdom comes in knowing that we are created by God to be uniquely and distinguishably beautiful. There is no one set standard of beauty. When we really realize this, we will stop comparing ourselves to others and be content with who God made us to be. Our race, sex, eye color, hair texture and color, height, and weight (although you can buy colored contacts and weave, color your hair, lose weight, and even change your sex these days) are all determined by our genes.

The question is, Who determines our genes? The answer is found in the Book of Jeremiah 1:5 that states, "Before I formed thee in the belly I knew thee; and before thou camest forth out of the womb I sanctified thee, and I ordained thee a prophet unto the nations (KJV). The Lord is speaking to the prophet Jeremiah and identifying the fact that He formed or divinely created him. Just as God formed Jeremiah, He forms us all. It is God who determines our genes! That is awesome to know, and the best part is God also ordains us for certain tasks that He assigns to us. He called Jeremiah to be a prophet to the nations, and the exciting thing is that He calls each of us to something! He forms us and equips us just for that task. God knows what race, gender, etc. that you needed to be in order to fulfill your destiny. Therefore, you are just who you are supposed to be, uniquely beautiful!

To be unique is to be original, one of a kind, rare, and unusual. When we accept the fact that we are not to be clones or cookie cutter images of one another, then maybe we can celebrate all the diverse cultures and the beauty that is found

You Are Beautiful: Unlocking Beauty from Within

in every race, shape, color, and size. God made each of us, and He doesn't make junk! We spend time and money to all wear the same designer clothes, perfumes, shoes, jewelry, etc. We are made to believe we have to wear a certain designer label or we are not fashionable. I don't know about you, but I realized a long time ago that it is not the clothes and accessories that make one unique; it is within the spirit of a person where the uniqueness resides, inside the heart.

You have to desire to be uniquely you, in order to radiate that uniqueness. If you just want to blend in and look like everyone else, then you probably have no clue as to who you really are. That is a normal part of growing and maturing, but at some point you must move past that and begin to understand who you are and that you are a genuine article. You might ask how you can mature into knowing who you are. That is a very good question that many people are afraid to admit they have. It all begins with getting to know the One who made you, the Lord God Almighty, as He manifests Himself through the blessed Trinity: Father, Son, and Holy Ghost. You must first believe in God and trust in Him. Then you must accept Jesus Christ as your personal Lord and Savior; after that the journey begins!

Just like the Apostle Paul, who was knocked off his high horse and blinded as he went about his misguided business (Acts 9), we too must sometimes be knocked into the place where we can hear the voice of the Lord calling. We must respond by crying out, "Who art thou Lord?" just as Saul, who was later to become Paul, did (Acts 9:5). It begins with getting to know who the Lord is; and then we can find out who we are through, in, and by Him.

The next question that Saul asked was, "Lord what will you have me to do?" (Acts 9:6) He realized that the Lord had an agenda and plan for his life, and he wanted to know what it was. That is precisely what we must do once the Lord gets our attention and we hear His voice and acknowledge who He is; we must then ask Him what He desires for us to do. After Saul asked the Lord what he must do, the Lord was able to set him apart and open his eyes to whom he was to become—the Apostle Paul, who wrote the majority of the New Testament Epistles. God is the only one that can truly open our eyes to who we are and who we are to become in Christ.

God will also change our names, just as He changed Saul's name to Paul. Saul means "desired," and Paul means "small or little." We all need a name change when we come to know who we really are. God "desired" Paul even when he was Saul and once he became Paul he had to make him "small" or "little" in his own eyes that God might become bigger. Paul had to decrease so that the Lord could increase! We must become aware of the fact that we are not what people have been calling us, especially in some of the rap songs that demean and devalue women. We realize that we are not "bitches" and "hoes"; we are women of God! I once was caught up in the vicious cycle of addiction to drugs and alcohol, and I had no clue to who I really was. I used to hang out in the clubs, and I received the nickname of Frosty. It wasn't until I surrendered my life to the Lord Jesus Christ that I understood who I was, according to what the word of God says, and not the "street committee!" I realized that I am indeed fearfully and wonderfully made. I also received a name change. Frosty was buried in the sea of forgetfulness, and my birth name, Rosalind which means "beautiful rose" in Spanish, took on greater value and significance. Ultimately God called me Delivered, Saved, and Free. Praise God, I have been drug and alcohol free for over twenty-years! Let God change your name!

Affirmations: "I am uniquely beautiful!"
"I am fearfully and wonderfully made!"

Dream Again

I had a dream last night, but it didn't last long;
In the dream, I was singing a song
About how in life things can go wrong;
But even then there is a chance to go on.
I had a dream last night about what love looks like,
And in the dream I thought about the plight of men and women
Caught up in a daze, purple haze, eyes all glazed, looking half crazed,
Walking and wandering through life unphased by all of the chaos and sin all around, looking for love in a world turned upside down.
I had a dream last night, but something had changed—
The tables had turned, and inside my head burned with the awareness and knowledge that life is for living and love is for loving and songs are for singing; and in the midst of it all my alarm clock started ringing.
I arose from my bed, shook my head, and thought about the things that I had reaped, and then it dawned on me that I wasn't really asleep!
For the first time in my life my eyes were wide open, and I was aware and awake to the things that make life worth living and time worth giving to the things that bring release and offer peace.
So whether awake or asleep, dream of a life filled with songs for the soul and love that makes whole whatever is broken.
Dream of hope and joy for better days ahead;
And when you dream, get out of your bed and bring to reality the things that were said!

CHAPTER 9

Beautiful Health

Unlocking Beauty from Within!

To be healthy is to be beautiful, no matter your gender, race, or religion, no matter your size, color, height, or zip code! That is really what we should be focusing on as a people, not merely on our physical appearance, but on our mental and physical health and well-being. If we spent more time and money on living healthy and less time on our self image, then we would feel better, look better, and spend less money on health care, including prescription drugs.

There is a health care crisis in the United States and abroad. In most third world countries it is stemming from war, unsanitary water, and lack of food. In the United States of America there are various issues that we face in relation to the health of our people. One issue is the high cost of health care. As a result, many Americans do not have health insurance and therefore are not privy to the medical care that is needed. As such, routine doctor visits and tests that can save lives and improve the overall quality of life are not available and the health of our nation suffers. Thank God that things are turning around slowly but surely in that area!

Another major issue is the fact that too many Americans are obese. Obesity is causing various diseases in our children and adults. In addition, cigarette smoking and the consumption of alcohol and illegal drugs are producing major illnesses and putting a strain on our health care system. Overeating, smoking, and using drugs and alcohol are causing everything from high blood pressure, diabetes, heart disease, lung cancer, and many other illnesses and diseases.

There are, however, things that we can do to improve our health on an individual basis. Studies show the importance of eating right and exercising in order to maintain optimum health. Nutrition plays an intricate role in determining whether one is healthy or not. When we eat balanced meals with the proper amounts of fruits and vegetables, our bodies feel and look better. Another issue that causes disease is irresponsible sexual intercourse, which often results in various sexually transmitted diseases, including HIV/AIDS. It is our responsibility to take care of our bodies, which are the temples of God (2 Corinthians 6:16). Whenever we take care of our temples by eating and exercising appropriately, as well as not engaging in sexual immorality, it produces good health, and that is beautiful!

There are principles found in the Bible that can help us to maintain good health. I have grouped **sanctification, preservation, prosperity, rest, hope, and prayer** and named them "God's Divine Healthcare Plan." The good thing is that you don't need health insurance to join God's health plan; all you need is God's assurance, which is faith!

God's Divine Health Plan

The Bible states, in I Thessalonians 5:23, "And the very God of peace sanctify you wholly; and I pray God your whole spirit and soul and body be preserved blameless unto the coming of our Lord Jesus Christ (KJV). The first part of the divine health care plan is **sanctification**. The Apostle Paul prays that the God of peace sanctify you wholly. The word for "sanctify," in this particular scripture is the Greek word *hagiazo* \hag·ee·ad·zo\; and it means "to render or acknowledge, or to be venerable or hallow, to separate from profane things and dedicate to God, consecrate things to God, dedicate people to God, to purify, to cleanse externally, to purify by expiation: free from the guilt of sin, to purify internally by renewing of the soul." In order to walk in divine health we first must allow God to sanctify us.

Many people believe that to be sanctified is to be a member of a particular church or denomination and wear long dresses and no make-up or jewelry. That is not sanctification according to God's word. That is a person's attempt to appear one way when, in fact, in many instances, he or she is another. Sanctification is greater than what you wear or don't wear. It's much deeper than that. To be sanctified is to be set apart by God, unto God, and away from the world, the flesh, and the devil. It is God that does the sanctifying when we allow Him to. Sanctification means to be separated from profane things. Profane things are those things that will defile or make vulgar your temple. This includes foods and substances that harm our bodies and produce sickness and disease. It means to be purified externally and internally.

One might ask, How does God do all of that? The answer is found in St. John 17:17, where Jesus is praying to the Father and petitions him to "Sanctify them through thy truth: thy word is truth (KJV). For "sanctify" in this particular scripture the writer uses the same Greek word identified above. We see very clearly that God sanctifies us or sets us apart through, by, and in His word. Whenever we allow the word to govern our lives and become the pathway or road map that we follow, we are automatically set apart unto God and away from the world, flesh, and devil! That is good news indeed! God desires to sanctify us "wholly," which simply means "completely." God does not want it to be a half-baked process. He desires for us to be completely set apart in every area—spirit, soul, and body—so that we may be preserved blameless.

The next thing that I would like to point out from I Thessalonians 5:23 is the fact that God will **preserve** us. That is another part of God's divine health care plan. In this particular scripture the Greek word for preserve is *tereo* \tay·reh·\; and it means "to attend to carefully, take care of, to guard, to keep, one in the state in which he is, to observe." I always say, "God will keep you if you want to be kept!' That is what He desires to do for each of His children, to attend to and take care of, guard and keep us in a state of divine health. The only things that you have to do are to trust God and abide in Him and allow His word to abide in you (St. John 15:7). Am I saying that you will never get sick? No! I cannot make that call; but I am saying that in sickness and in health, God will keep and take care of His children. I am a living witness of that!

In the Book, 3 John 2, the Bible states, "Beloved, I wish above all things that thou mayest prosper and be in health, even as thy soul prospereth" (KJV). In the referenced scripture, the Greek word for "prosper" is *euodoo* \yoo·od·o·o\; and it means "to grant a prosperous and expeditious journey, to lead by a direct and easy way, to grant a successful issue, to cause to prosper, to prosper, be successful." **Prosperity** is another part of God's divine health care plan. God desires to prosper you. That includes success in every area.

One of the reasons for that is because one of the major causes of sickness and disease is poverty. When one does not have enough resources to provide adequate food and nutrition, shelter, etc., it can take a toll on one's health. The living conditions of abject poverty often consist of unsanitary conditions, which are the breeding ground for all types of harmful bacteria and infections. You might ask, "Do I have to be prosperous to be healthy?" The answer is, "Of course not," but it is God's plan for your life for you to prosper and be in good health. Prosperity and good health go hand in hand. You probably can think of many scenarios where wealthy people have sickness and disease. I am not talking about just having money. Money cannot buy good health or prevent diseases, and true prosperity is not just about having an abundance of resources. We see very rich people who have terminal illnesses, mental and physical diseases just like poorer people, all of the time. What I am saying is that it is God's desire and idea for His children to prosper and be in good health. In God there is a strong correlation between the two. They go hand in hand like two peas in a pod, and that is good news! Let God prosper you and give you good health.

The next part of God's divine health care plan that I would like us to look at is **rest**. God desires to give rest to His people, and the reason is that our bodies need to have the chance to regroup and recharge. Simply getting the proper amount of rest can make a tremendous difference in our brain's ability to function properly, and rest also reduces stress. Stress is a big factor in many diseases. When we are worried and anxious, we are subject to "dis-ease," or disease. Often, in our fast, busy, multi-tasking lifestyles, we neglect our need for simple rest and relaxation.

The Bible states, in Matthew 11:28, "Come unto me, all ye that labour and are heavy laden, and I will give you **rest**" (KJV). In this particular scripture, rest is \an·ap·ow·o\; and it means "to cause or permit one to cease from any movement or labour in order to recover and collect his strength, to give rest, refresh, to give one's self rest, take rest, to keep quiet, of calm and patient expectation." As we come to the Lord, we can receive strength and be refreshed in the presence of God. So many times we try to carry our burdens on our shoulders, and they cause us not to be able to sleep, and we toss and turn all night long.

The good news is that God desires to take our yokes and burdens, so we can have rest. In Matthew 11:29, the Bible states, "Take my yoke upon you, and learn of me; for I am meek and lowly in heart: and ye shall find **rest** unto your souls." In this particular scripture, another Greek word is used for "rest," *anapausis* \an·ap·ow·sis\; and it means, "intermission, cessation of any motion, business or labour, rest, recreation." When we take the Lord's yoke, He takes ours. There is a heavenly exchange and we can find relief and rest for our souls, which are our minds, wills, and emotions. That rest includes taking time out from our normal routine, and it also means recreation. When we recreate, God refreshes, restores, and re-creates us. God wants us to have fun and enjoy our lives! That is a key to maintaining divine health. That is good news, indeed, because I don't know about you, but I have much responsibility; and sometimes it can be too much for me to bear. I thank God it is not too much for me and the Lord. Aren't you glad that He is willing to give you rest? Take God up on that offer and receive the gift of rest from the Lord!

Another very important part of God's divine health care plan, is **hope.** Hope has been said to be pregnant expectancy. In Hebrews 11:1, the Bible states, "Now faith is the substance of things hoped for, the evidence of things not seen" (KJV). It is so important to hope until you cannot have faith without it. Hope will give you a reason to get up in the morning and continue to press on. Hope will give you a reason not to give up and to try again even after you fail. Hope will heal your disappointments and cover your failures because with hope, there is always tomorrow. Hope speaks to your future while in the midst of your today, and hope will propel you into your destiny.

My trademark saying is, "As long as there is breath in your body, there is hope!" This implies that you have another chance to get it right. Hopelessness causes one to give up on dreams and not really live the abundant life that Jesus came to give each of us. Hope is extremely important, especially to your mental and emotional health. The Bible states, in the Book of Proverbs 13:12, that Hope deferred maketh the heart sick: but when the desire cometh, it is a tree of life (KJV). In this particular scripture, the Hebrew word *mashak* \maw·shak\; is translated as "deferred"; and it means "to drag along, lead along, drag or lead off, draw down, to be drawn out, be postponed, be deferred." I have found this to be true in so many instances in my life, whenever it seemed like the thing that I was hoping for was taking too long to come. Have you ever felt that way before? It certainly does make your heart sick. The good news is that if you just hold on to God's unchanging hand, you will find out, as Job did in the Bible; that God will give you double for your trouble if you just wait on Him! So many times people give up hope and stop trying right before the breakthrough comes.

Even in the midst of trouble, hope can be your way out. In the Book of Hosea 2:15, the Bible states, "And I will give her her vineyards from thence, and the valley of Achor for a door of hope: and she shall sing there, as in the days of her youth, and as in the day when she came up out of the land of Egypt"

(KJV). According to Easton's *Bible Dictionary*, "Achor," in the referenced scripture, means "trouble, a valley near Jericho, so called in consequence of the trouble which the sin of Achan caused Israel (Josh. 7:24,26). The expression "valley of Achor" probably became proverbial for **that which caused trouble**, and when Isaiah (Isa. 65:10) refers to it, he uses it in this sense: "The valley of Achor, a place for herds to lie down in;" i.e., that which had been a source of calamity would become a source of blessing. Hosea also (Hos. 2:15) uses the expression in the same sense: "The valley of Achor for a door of hope;" i.e., trouble would be turned into joy, despair into hope.

God will turn your trouble into joy, but you must access it through the door of hope. When you walk through the door of hope, you come into the place of trust and faith in God to know that He has you in the palm of His hands and that trouble won't last always. A person who has hope is a beautiful person because hope lifts one up above whatever the situation is that he or she is going through and it causes one to shine with expectation and become pregnant with promise.

Prayer is the vehicle used to access your divine health and healing. Medical research has proven time and time again the importance of prayer as it relates to the health and well-being being of a person. Studies show that people who pray are generally healthier and that prayer plays a major role in the healing process. The word of God gives clear instructions as to the importance of prayer as it relates to sickness, as seen in the Book of St. James 5:14-16: "Is any sick among you? let him call for the elders of the church; and let them pray over him, anointing him with oil in the name of the Lord: And the prayer of faith shall save the sick, and the Lord shall raise him up; and if he have committed sins, they shall be forgiven him. Confess your faults one to another, and pray one for another, that ye may be healed" (KJV). Prayer is an intricate part of the healing process because God's power is released through prayer. Prayer is our access code in God's divine Health Care plan. Through prayer we access our sanctification, preservation, prosperity, rest, and hope.

Not only is divine health available through Christ; but divine healing is available as well, and that is beautiful! When Jesus died on the cross for our sins, He took on all of our sicknesses and diseases as well; and the Bible says "by his stripes we were healed" (I Peter 2:24). That is good news because even if we are afflicted with a disease, God is ready, willing, and able to heal us by the blood of Jesus! By faith, we can apply the finished work that Jesus did on the cross and receive our healing. There are countless testimonies found in the Bible of "Jesus going about doing good and healing all who were oppressed by the devil" (Acts 10:38 KJV).

We also find in the New Testament church that is identified in the Book of Acts that the healing continued through the believers in Christ. The healing continues even today because there are testimonies everyday of God's healing anointing being released, resulting in bodies being healed! God heals supernaturally through prayer and laying on of hands. God also heals naturally through doctors and medical science. Either way it is God's doing and it is marvelous in our eyes!

Affirmations: **"I am covered under God's Divine Health Care Plan!"**

"I am healed by the stripes of Jesus!"

Where Is Hope?

Hope is found in the Breath that I Breathe,
In the Stars in the Sky, and in the Cool of the Breeze.
Hope is found in a Baby's Cry; or Tears rolling down the Eye
Of one who knows that every good thing Flows from the Heart of God.
Hope is found in the Birds that Sing, in the Grass as it Grows,
In the Smell of a Rose, in the Dew as it settles upon the Ground.
Hope can be found in the middle of Pain, in the Streets of Frustration, and in the Home of the Name that is above every Name!
Hope is found when you Hear the Name, Think the Name, or Say the Name—it's all the Same!
Because, Jesus IS HOPE!

CHAPTER 10

Kingdom Beauty

Unlocking Beauty from Within!

As discussed earlier, we realize that true beauty comes from inside; it is more than skin deep; and it comes from God. That is why the Bible states in I Samuel 16:7 "But the LORD said unto Samuel, Look not on his countenance, or on the height of his stature; because I have refused him: for the LORD seeth not as man seeth; for man looketh on the outward **appearance**, but the LORD looketh on the heart" (KJV). In this passage, the scripture is referring to the time when Samuel went to anoint David as the next king of Israel after King Saul was stripped of his kingship by God. Jesse paraded all of his sons in front of Samuel, and they appeared to be king material. They were all big, strong, tall, and handsome. Samuel was very impressed by these young men and was ready to make one of them king based upon their outward appearance. That is when the Lord stepped in with the above scripture saying basically not to judge by how they look on the outside, but to look at their hearts.

The heart is the place of true beauty. The heart consists of our spirit and soul. It is the center of our being. It is the control station of our lives. That is why the Bible says that we are to keep or guard our hearts with all diligence, because out of our hearts flow the issues of life (Proverbs 4:23). It is important to keep our hearts free from hatred, anger, bitterness, the failure to forgive, and other toxic emotions, which have a tendency to make us ugly inside. Whenever we are harboring negative energy and emotions, we are placed in a state of turmoil. That turmoil can be seen on the outside no matter how we cover it up. It will appear and blemish our beauty every time. The best thing that we can do to insure that our beauty is flowing from inside out is to grasp the concept of the kingdom of God and fill our temples with beauty that will shine for the entire world to see.

   I love nature, and one morning while walking around Grande Lake in the City of Orlando, FL, the Lord began to talk to me about kingdom beauty. It was at the breaking of day and kind of cloudy as I walked. There was a gentle breeze blowing on this July morning. As I looked at the rolling hills of green that overlooked the golf course, I was struck by the peace that surrounded me. I closed my eyes and internalized the peace and serenity that I was feeling at that moment. I prayed a quiet prayer asking God to please help me keep the peace that I was feeling after going back home to Tallahassee, FL.

   It was then that God began to speak to me about the kingdom of God being a place of beauty on the inside of us. The Bible states in Luke 17:21, "Neither shall they say, Lo here! or, lo there! for, behold, the **kingdom** of God is within you" (KJV). And in Romans 14:17, "For the **kingdom** of God is not meat and drink; but righteousness, and peace, and joy in the Holy Ghost" (KJV). In these specific scriptures the Greek word for "kingdom" is *basileia* \bas·il·i·ah\; and it means "royal power, kingship, dominion, rule, not to be confused with an actual kingdom but rather the right or authority to rule over a kingdom, of the royal power of Jesus as the triumphant Messiah, of the royal power and dignity conferred on Christians in the Messiah's kingdom, a kingdom, the territory subject to the rule of a king, used in the N.T. to refer to the reign of the Messiah."

   God's royal power and dominion rest inside of those who believe in the Lordship of Jesus Christ. His kingdom inside of us manifests in righteousness, peace, and joy. Whenever we behold beauty clothed in righteousness, peace, and joy, we can bring it on the inside of us and experience the pleasure of adorning our temples. It is much like decorating your home. You see things that you like, which will bring joy to look at and create a certain atmosphere, so you purchase the items and bring them home. Well, the Lord was saying to me that we have the ability to behold the beauty and peace that is found in nature and bring it into our kingdom and decorate our temples by memorizing, internalizing, and meditating on what we have seen and experienced. God created us to have the ability to go back there at anytime through prayer and release the same peace and beauty that we experienced the first time we beheld the object of beauty.

That is why it is very important to surround yourself with beauty and peace. You must make a conscious effort to not just see beautiful things like the sunrise and sunset, the ocean, the mountains, the stars and moon, the trees and flowers of the world and then forget about what you have seen. No, you must drink it in so to speak. Let it get inside of you so that when you close your eyes, you still see the beauty and experience the peace, love, and joy all over again. That is powerful! And that is kingdom beauty that will radiate from inside of you as you fill your temple with the beauty of nature.

There have been seasons in my life when I know that if I had not spent time filling my temple with peace by spending time with God in nature, I would have been stressed out because of the circumstances that were taking place in my life. During a particularly trying time in my life, I would sit for hours in the woods just beholding God's beauty in nature. I was experiencing tremendous persecution, but it all went away as I sat still and quiet alone with God. Peace flooded my heart, and it was there that God birthed the gift of poetry. I began to write poems and release what I was feeling inside. My first collection was called "Poems of Spring." That is why I equate my poetry with beauty, because it is birthed out of a beautiful place inside and out.

Affirmations: **"My heart is a place of beauty!"**
"The kingdom of God is inside of me!"

Rosalind Y. Tompkins

I Cannot Be Shaken

There is a quaking going on:
If I'm not mistaken, everything around is being shaken!
People losing homes left and right,
Banking institutions crumbling fast,
Gas prices up and down and Wall Street crashed,
Job security is a thing of the past!
There is a quaking going on:
If I'm not mistaken everything around is being shaken!
Husbands and wives on the split,
War going on endlessly,
Teen-agers having sex recklessly,
People wondering how this could be,
Living in the twenty-first century,
Life was supposed to be about unity.
Instead, we spent time acquiring things,
Houses, cars, and diamond rings.
We just wanted to be living large—
The only problem is who's in charge.
What we really didn't know
Is that it is the creditors that we owe;
Now this whole thing is about to blow,
Like a big fat fiery Volcano!
There is a quaking going on
If I'm not mistaken, everything around is being shaken!
Things that cannot be shaken are holding on:
The Kingdom of God is still growing strong!
I cannot be shaken!

CHAPTER 11

Beauty Transformation

Unlocking Beauty from Within!

We live in a society that is fascinated by makeovers. We have talk and reality television shows dedicated to making over our bodies, our homes, our cars, our finances, and everything else. Makeover shows are some of the most popular shows ever. I can understand, because it does feel good to go into a retail store and sit at the cosmetic counter and allow someone to put make-up and lipstick on you and style your hair. It even helps if you have a new outfit, new earrings, and new shoes as well. You look and feel good inside and out the whole time you are made up. You want to go around all of your friends and family so they can see you; and you might even go and take a portrait photograph, just to have a picture of remembrance to hang on your wall.

It also feels good to lose weight and have a new sized body. You look good and feel good from head to toe! That is all well and good; but the Lord is interested in something much deeper, and that is transformation. Man can make you over, but only God can transform you! Transformation is an inside job that will show up on the outside; and there will be a true change in your life, not just your appearance. Transformation lasts while makeovers may not. Inevitably you will have to wipe the make-up off and take the clothes off. In many cases where there is weight loss, you may even end up putting the pounds back on with more!

The Bible states in 2 Corinthians 5:17, "Therefore if any man be in Christ, he is a new creature: old things are passed away; behold, all things are become new." In this particular scripture, the Greek word for "creature" is *ktisis* \ktis·is\; and it means; creation, after a rabbinical usage (by which a man converted from idolatry to Judaism was called).

God wants us to become new creatures. He is not so much interested in us looking the part as He is in us becoming like Him. In other words, man attempts to change the outer appearance while inwardly there is no real change. We may look different but we are still the same on the inside.

God's makeover is transformation, and that includes becoming a new man. In the Book of Ephesians 4:20-24, it states, "But ye have not so learned Christ; If so be that ye have heard him, and have been taught by him, as the truth is in Jesus: That ye put off concerning the former conversation the old man, which is corrupt according to the deceitful lusts; And **be renewed in the spirit of your mind**; And that ye put on the new man, which after God is created in righteousness and true holiness" (KJV). Again in Colossians 3:9-11, the Bible states, "Lie not one to another, seeing that ye have put off the old man with his deeds; And have put on the new man, **which is renewed in knowledge after the image of him that created him**: Where there is neither Greek nor Jew, circumcision nor uncircumcision, Barbarian, Scythian, bond nor free: but Christ is all, and in all" (KJV).

The new man is what God wants to change or transform us into. The new man does not live, think, or act the way he did before Christ. It is in Christ that we are transformed into the new man. But there must be a renewal process that takes place in our minds. That is why the above scriptures state that we need "to be renewed in the spirit of our minds" and "renewed in knowledge after the image of Christ." To be renewed is "to be made new spiritually, to restore to existence, and to make extensive changes in." The renewing of the mind is one way that transformation happens. It takes place in the mind as we allow the Holy Spirit to recreate our thought patterns and belief systems through the word of God.

The Bible states in Romans 12:1-2, "I beseech you therefore, brethren, by the mercies of God, that ye present your bodies a living sacrifice, holy, acceptable unto God, which is your reasonable service. And be not conformed to this world: but be ye **transformed** by the **renewing of your mind,** that ye may prove what is that good, and acceptable, and perfect, will of God"(KJV). In this particular scripture the Greek word for "transformation" is *metamorphoo* \met·am·or·fo·o; and it means "to change into another form, to transform, to transfigure."

Christ's appearance was changed and was resplendent with divine brightness on the mount of transfiguration. This particular Greek word occurs four times in the New Testament. *Metamorphoo* is translated as "transfigure" twice, "transform" once, and "change" once. We will look at the other three times it is used now. In the Book of Matthew 17:1-2, the Bible states, "And after six days Jesus taketh Peter, James, and John his brother, and bringeth them up into an high mountain apart, And was **transfigured** before them: and his face did shine as the sun, and his raiment was white as the light" (KJV). (This same account is found in Mark 9:2.)

The fourth time that we see *metamorphoo* used in the New Testament scriptures is in 2 Corinthians 3:18 (as stated in Chapter 6, "Clothed In Beauty): "But we all, with open face beholding as in a glass the glory of the Lord, are **changed** into the same image from glory to glory, even as by the Spirit of the Lord." *Metamorphoo* is the change that takes place during a metamorphosis. "Metamorphosis" is a Latin word that we are more familiar with; and it means "change of physical form, structure, or substance especially by supernatural means." We are familiar with this term because it describes the process that takes place when a caterpillar becomes a butterfly. There is a structural change that takes place, which allows the insect to literally go from crawling on the ground to flying in the sky with wings. That is a beautiful metaphor to help us see exactly what the Lord desires. He desires for us to get our wings and fly in the Spirit! We can do that when we allow the transformation process to take place.

Renewing of the mind and moving from glory to glory will bring about lasting true transformation. In the account of scripture where Jesus went up on the mount of transfiguration, he was literally changed into another right before the eyes of Peter, James, and John. The glory cloud enveloped Him; and His face shone bright as the light. The same happened to Moses whenever he spent time on the mountain in the presence of the Lord. When he came down off the mountain, his face shone so bright until the Israelites had him put a veil over his face (2 Corinthians 3:6-17). Well, the veil has been rent through Christ's finished work on the cross; and now, by the Spirit of Christ, we can all behold the glory of God and be changed into His image!

Transformation is a process. It is not going to happen overnight. Just like the caterpillar has to go into the cocoon for a season before he is changed into the butterfly, we too must go through seasons of waiting on the Lord. The process is not easy. We live in a microwave society that wants everything quick, fast, and in a hurry. True transformation is not going to happen overnight just because someone laid hands on you and you felt God's glory and fell to the floor in church; that doesn't mean you are changed. You have to do the work in order for transformation to take place. Yes, God's glory changes us and helps up to go to another place; but the other part of transformation is the renewing of the mind, and that takes work and time. That takes you actually reading, studying, and hearing the word of God. That takes putting what you hear into practice. That takes stumbling and falling and getting back up and trying again all by the grace of God.

That is why many Christians are not transformed and choose to live carnal lives. They do not want to go through the process and do the work, but I am here to tell you that it is worth it! You can move from glory to glory; and the things that you used to think were right, you will see that they are wrong, no matter what the world says. After you overcome in one area, God will show you other areas that need to be renewed; it is an ongoing process that is powerful!

It is powerful because you can see your growth and be encouraged to keep growing and going higher. I have found that the more growth, the more blessings that God will bestow upon you because you can handle it. Many times we are not blessed in a certain area because God knows that the blessing would kill us. I have seen people be blessed prematurely with worldly possessions, a particular relationship, or a certain position, only to lose everything because their minds were not being renewed, and therefore they could not handle the blessings.

God is inviting us to go up higher in our thinking and our walk with Him. He desires for us to stop scratching around with the chickens on the ground and get our wings to fly high with the eagles! We can do that when we allow our thinking to be elevated to think as God does. The Bible says in Isaiah 55:7-11, "Seek ye the LORD while he may be found, call ye upon him while he is near: Let the wicked forsake his way, and the unrighteous man his thoughts: and let him return unto the LORD, and he will have mercy upon him; and to our God, for he will abundantly pardon. For my thoughts are not your thoughts, neither are your ways my ways, saith the LORD. For as the heavens are higher than the earth, so are my ways higher than your ways, and my thoughts than your thoughts. For as the rain cometh down, and the snow from heaven, and returneth not thither, but watereth the earth, and maketh it bring forth and bud, that it may give seed to the sower, and bread to the eater: So shall my word be that goeth forth out of my mouth: it shall not return unto me void, but it shall accomplish that which I please, and it shall prosper in the thing whereto I sent it."

We don't have to wonder what God's thoughts or ways are because God's thoughts and ways are found in the word of God. When we search the scriptures, we can see that they are indeed higher than our thoughts. Our minds and the eyes of our understanding have to be opened up by the Holy Spirit in order for us to be able to grasp the height and depth of God's word. As we allow that to take place, we are being transformed. The enemy hates to see this happening; and he will do anything and everything that he can to stop, block, kill, still, and destroy. That is why we find that the Bible states in 2 Corinthians 10:4, "For the weapons of our warfare are not carnal, but mighty through God to the pulling down of strong holds, casting down imaginations, and every high thing that exalteth itself against the knowledge of God, and bringing into captivity every thought to the obedience of Christ, and having in a readiness to revenge all disobedience, when your obedience is fulfilled." (KJV)

In this passage, the Greek word for "weapons" is *hoplon* \ hop·lon\; and it means "any tool or implement for preparing a thing, arms used in warfare, weapons, an instrument." The tools that we use to walk in victory over the enemy's attacks are the sword of the Spirit, which is the spoken word of God, prayer, and praise. The strongholds are the thoughts and belief systems that try to exalt themselves above the truth of God's word. The battlefield is the mind. When we consistently wage war against the onslaught of terror that takes place in our minds and allow the word of God preeminence over anything else, then we can maintain our transformation.

Therefore, when we start to think thoughts, such as, "I am ugly, nobody wants me, I am fat, I am going to always be alone," then we must take the word and begin to speak it over our lives. We can say things like, "I am beautiful, I am created in the image of God, God will never leave me nor forsake me, God will give me the desires of my heart, I am fearfully and wonderfully made," and "I can do all things through Christ who strengthens me." Speak the word and believe what you say, and the enemy will run every time, and you will have the victory!

Sometimes you need to have others speak over your life to remind you of who you are. That is why it is very important who you let speak into your life. You need friends who will affirm the word in you and not agree with the lies of the enemy. You need people who will build you up and not tear you down. You need people in your life, who when you can't pray and speak the word, will do it for you; and when they can't, you will do it for them. When that is in place, you will see not just yourself, but families, churches, communities, and nations being transformed!

Affirmations: **"I am renewing my mind through the Word of God!"**
"I am being transformed by God!"

Rosalind Y. Tompkins

Transformation

The caterpillar wonders why she can't fly,
Crawling around with her head hanging down, wearing a frown.
Inside she sees wings, like none she's ever seen,
Flying high through the sky among the trees;
But in reality, day after day, she crawls around, dodging birds of prey;
But inside she sees wings, like none she's ever seen,
Flying high through the sky among the trees.
One day as she sees she believes that the wings belong to her.
She pictures herself flying, and a process begins trying to make her become what she was born to be;
The process of transformation is finally taking her off the ground and into the trees,
Flying high through the sky with wings like none she's ever seen;
But now she possesses and her soul caresses life as it is supposed to be—
No more crawling around with her head hanging down, wearing a frown;
She now has her wings to fly high through the sky way up in the trees!
You may be like that caterpillar living your life crawling around with your head hanging down, wearing a frown;
Jesus came to give you your wings, so you, too, can fly, high, through the sky way up in the trees;
Look inside where Christ resides and see the new creation that you were born again to be;
Allow the process of transformation to begin taking you off the ground and into the trees,
Flying high in the Spirit with wings like none you've ever seen;
But now you possess and your soul can caress life and that more Abundantly!

CHAPTER 12

Beauty Affirmations

Unlocking Beauty from Within!

Many people do not realize that an intricate part of a good beauty regimen is words. Words help to create our world, and the words that we speak about ourselves and to ourselves have great power. Just as God spoke and the world was created, what we speak helps to determine the type of world that we live in. As a matter of fact, the Bible states, in the Book of Proverbs 18:21, "Death and life arc in the **power** of the tongue: and they that love it shall eat the fruit thereof (KJV). In this particular scripture the Hebrew word for "power" is *yad* \yawd\; and it means "hand, hand (of man), strength, power." Death and life are in your hands based upon the words that you speak. Now that is powerful! That is why I included affirmations at the end of each chapter of the book—because as you begin to speak these positive words over yourself and about yourself, for your ears to hear, your creative "hand," or power, will be released to manifest the truth of your beauty for the entire world to see!

To "affirm" means "to assert positively and declare to be a fact." Whenever you read the affirmations listed below, do not just say them, but affirm them with power. Declare and decree that they are so. Say them like you mean them. As you declare and decree it, you shall believe it and receive it because all of heaven will back up your words. As it says in Job 22:28, "Thou shalt also decree a thing, and it shall be established unto thee: and the light shall shine upon thy ways" (KJV).

I recommend that you look in the mirror and speak at least three beauty affirmations a day, one in the morning, one around noon, and one more before going to bed at night.

Beauty Affirmations:
1. "I am beautiful!"
2. "Today I will smile!"
3. "Today I will praise the Lord!"
4. "My feet are beautiful!"
5. "I walk By faith and not by sight!"
6. "I am a doer of God's Word!"
7. "Today I am filled with wonder!"
8. "Today I will laugh!"
9. "God loves me!"
10. "I love God!"
11. "I love others!
12. "I love myself!"
13. "I am created in the image of God!"
14. "I am godly!"
15. "My body belongs to God!"
16. "I will glorify God with my body!"
17. "I will glorify God with my spirit!"
18. "My body is a temple of God!"
19. "The Holy Spirit lives in me!"
20. "God makes everything beautiful in His time!"
21. "I am clothed with God's glory!"
22. "I am filled with God's spirit!"

23. "I will share my wounds with God!"
24. "I will share my wounds with others!"
25. "My wounds represent my experiences!"
26. "My wounds are beautiful!"
27. "I am uniquely beautiful!"
28. "I am fearfully and wonderfully made!"
29. "I am covered under God's Divine Health Care Plan!"
30. "I am healed by the stripes of Jesus!"
31. "My heart is a place of beauty!"
32. "The kingdom of God is inside of me!"
33. "I am renewing my mind through the Word of God!"
34. "I am being transformed by God!"

Rosalind Y. Tompkins

Can We Talk?

Can we talk until the wee hours of the morning and until the sun begins to peep upon the horizon?
Can we talk until light becomes dark and dark becomes light?
Can we talk morning, noon, and night, even when we aren't saying a word?
Can we talk until life becomes clear and time stands still?
Can we talk through the pain and the shame until we reach down so deep that we touch the stars?
Can we talk? Can we talk? Can we talk?
Can we talk until we run out of words to say and our heart beats speak and our knees grow weak and we create a new language of love?
Can we talk just for fun until we become one?
Can we talk? Can we talk? Can we talk?

CHAPTER 13

The Beauty of Wisdom

Unlocking Beauty from Within!

The Bible states in Proverbs 31:30, "Favour is deceitful, and beauty is **vain**: but a woman that feareth the LORD, she shall be praised (KJV). In this passage, the Hebrew word for "vain" is *hebel, or* (rarely, abs.), *habel* \heh·bel\; and it means "vapour, breath." Beauty is like a vapor or breath that is fleeting and is here today and gone tomorrow. The fear of the Lord, however, is the beginning of wisdom (Psalm 111:10); and that is what brings praise, not beauty alone. Wisdom is learning to reverence and honor the Lord in all our ways. Wisdom causes one to look beautiful. The Book of Ecclesiastes 8:1 states, "Who is like the wise man? Who knows the explanation of things? Wisdom brightens a man's face and changes its hard appearance (NIV). Wisdom will take the hard edge off of your appearance. That is powerful!

We must learn to apply wisdom, as we would make-up, as part of our daily beauty routine. In order to do that, we first must realize that true wisdom comes only from God. When we read the word of God, we are receiving wisdom. The more of the word of God that we read, understand, and apply to our daily lives, the more wisdom we have; and the more wisdom we have, the better we look. I have taken from each chapter Words of Wisdom **(WOW),** which I list below as a way to capture in a nutshell the essence of what each chapter is saying. Use the words of wisdom as a way to meditate on God's principles of beauty. Do this daily as a part of your beauty regime and watch your face change and take on a soft, elegant, inner glow that comes from obtaining wisdom.

WOW!

A humble or lowly attitude will cause God to pour out His glory and thus make you truly beautiful no matter what your outer appearance may be!

Do a good deed for someone in need and watch how your beauty rises from within!

There is a certain aura about a truly beautiful woman with inward beauty that cannot be attributed to her clothes, hair, jewelry, or make-up!

You can be saved and still look sexy!

Although you may not be beautiful to everyone, you can rest assured that you are beautiful to God!

A smile does more for the face than a ton of make-up or jewelry ever could!

Whenever you carry the good news, your feet are beautiful!

You become what you behold!

If you look into the mirror of the word of God long enough, you will become beautiful indeed, all the way from your head to your feet!

WOW!

Whenever you possess the characteristics and qualities of wonder, humor, kindness, love, and godliness, you are beautiful from the inside out; and it doesn't matter if you are one or one hundred and one, you are beautiful!

When you are genuinely surprised and amazed with the freshness of life in the Holy Spirit, it causes your eyes to sparkle; and it produces a childlike expression that is beautiful indeed!

Kindness is a beautiful quality that looks good on anyone!

To be kind is to be beautiful no matter how old you are!

Kindness looks good on toddlers as well as senior citizens and everyone in between!

When you don't look or feel your best, look for the humor in your situation. Sometimes, just looking in the mirror and seeing how silly you look will cause you to laugh at yourself!

Laugh with, not at, others!

The true essence of love is beautiful!

WOW!

The one who loves and the object of the one loving are both made beautiful by love!

When you love as God loves, you realize that the love is coming forth from you, not based upon what the other person does or doesn't do, but upon the love that is on the inside of you!

We can look all around at God's creation and see love!

We can look at one another and see beauty exuding from the eyes and hearts of our fellowmen!

We are created in the image of God. If the image is beautiful, then we know that the genuine article, God, is exceedingly beautiful; and therefore, to be godly is to be beautiful!

To live a life set apart for the Master's use is beautiful!

We are to live a life of worship and holiness unto the Lord, so that His beauty will shine through us!

We must flee fornication and run into God!

Rosalind Y. Tompkins

WOW!

It is indeed pleasant, delightful, sweet, lovely, and beautiful to be in the presence of God!

We know that what covers our body is skin, and we are created in God's image; therefore, what covers God's body is His skin, and that happens to be His glory, and God's glory is beautiful!

God's splendor, brightness, magnificence, excellence, majesty, etc. resides in you as a child of God; and that is the true beauty that will cause you to shine brighter than the stars on a dark night!

God wants to clothe all of His creation in His glory!

There is a brightness that resides upon a person that is clothed in God's glory, an inner glow that shines brightly through the eyes of one who is filled with God's Spirit!

It's not so much about what you have on; it's about who you have inside of you!

Eyes are windows to the heart and soul of a person; therefore, it is important that your eyes are single, whole, and sound so that they may reflect the light of God's glory!

WOW!

If you just see my beauty and not my scars, then you have not really seen me because my wounds are a part of my beauty!

Your scars are beautiful because they represent a part of your life that you experienced and by the grace of God you survived! Your wounds are a reminder of God's goodness to you!

Comparison is one of the biggest problems that we have as it relates to our perception of beauty!

There is no one set standard of beauty. When we really realize this, we will stop comparing ourselves to others and be content with who God made us to be!

You must first believe in God and trust in Him; then, you must accept Jesus Christ as your personal Lord and Savior. After that, the journey begins!

God is the only one that can truly open our eyes to who we are and who we are to become in Christ!

WOW!

Let God change your name!

To be healthy is to be beautiful, no matter your gender, race, or religion, no matter your size, color, height, or zip code!

Taking care of our temples by eating and exercising appropriately, as well as not engaging in sexual intercourse outside of marriage, produces good health; and that is beautiful!

The principles of sanctification, preservation, prosperity, rest, hope, and prayer are God's Divine Health Care Plan!

You don't need health insurance to join God's health plan; all you need is God's assurance, which is faith!

Prayer is the vehicle used to access your divine health and healing!

Prayer is our access code in God's Divine Health Care Plan. We access our sanctification, preservation, prosperity, rest, and hope through prayer!

WOW!

A person who has hope is a beautiful person because hope lifts you up above whatever the situation is that you are going through, and it causes you to shine with expectation and become pregnant with promise!

Not only is divine health available through Christ, but divine healing is available as well; and that is beautiful!

The heart is the place of true beauty!

Rosalind Y. Tompkins

The best thing that we can do to insure that our beauty is flowing from inside out is to grasp the concept of the kingdom of God and fill our temples with beauty that will shine for the entire world to see.

Whenever we behold beauty clothed in righteousness, peace, and joy, we can bring it to the inside of us and experience the pleasure of adorning our temples. It is much like decorating your home.

Man can make you over, but only God can transform you!

Transformation is an inside job that will show up on the outside; and there will be a true change in your life, not just your appearance!

WOW!

Renewing of the mind and moving from glory to glory will bring about lasting true transformation!

Transformation is a process!

True transformation is not going to happen overnight just because someone laid hands on you, and you fell to the floor; that doesn't mean you are changed!

You have to do the work in order for transformation to take place!

After you overcome in one area, God will show you other areas that need to be renewed; it is an ongoing process that is powerful!

Our minds and the eyes of our understanding have to be opened up by the Holy Spirit in order for us to be able to grasp the height and depth of God's word.

The tools that we use to walk in victory over the enemy's attacks are the sword of the Spirit, which is the spoken word of God, prayer, and praise!

The battlefield is the mind!

WOW!

When we consistently wage war against the onslaught of terror that takes place in our minds and allow the word of God preeminence over anything else, then we can maintain our transformation!

You need people in your life who, when you can't pray and speak the word, will do it for you; and when they can't, you will do it for them. When that is in place, you will see not just yourself, but families, churches, communities, and nations being transformed!

Death and life are in your hands based upon the words that you speak!

The fear of the Lord is the beginning of wisdom; and that is what brings praise, not beauty alone!

Wisdom causes one to look beautiful!

Wisdom will take the hard edge off of your appearance!

We must learn to apply wisdom as we would apply make-up—as part of our daily beauty routine!

Rosalind Y. Tompkins

Powerful

Crushing, Rushing, Majesty, the voice of the Lord speaks.
From the depths of the sea, the ocean is calling me to a place that I have never been.
The power of the ocean surrounds me.
Crushing, Rushing, Majesty, the voice of the Lord speaks.
Inside of me, I hear the call of the sea; the ocean sings a melody of powerful possibilities.
I rock, I sway, and I'm lulled away as an infant in a cradle or a baby in the womb.
I am engulfed by the sea; the ocean speaks to me.
Crushing, Rushing, Majesty, the voice of the Lord speaks.

Water & Sand

From the ocean to the desert, God made this great land.
He's given us the knowledge and wisdom to understand.
It's not about houses, cars, or material things,
but it's all about love and the hope that it brings
for new life and possibilities that expand with each and every day,
From the sky to the sea, from the forest to you and me, there is an ocean, there is a desert, and there are mountains and valleys.
Clear as the sky on a warm summer's day,
sweet as the mango ripened in the sun,
hard as the pearl enclosed in the oyster,
grand as the mind set on finding answers
Is the life filled with oceans and deserts!

Poems of Africa

The Motherland

I can hear the sound of the beat of the drums in the atmosphere even in the airplane.

The beat of a people with passion too deep for words and pain that leaves one speechless and without air to breathe;

I sense the zeal of a people with nothing to lose, but everything to gain; and as they call on Jesus' name, he takes away the shame.

I know my life will never be the same, even though my feet have not yet touched African soil; the Holy Spirit met me in the air, and I do declare that I am home!

Rosalind Y. Tompkins

Lost Luggage

Welcome to Kenya, a country of greatness—busy, friendly, with internet and modern rooms.
A time to pray and listen for what is to come later:
Crusade!
Swarms of people filled the park; in the midst of it all, a very dark presence came on the stage—
People acting out and souls possessed, in distress, fighting, crawling, and crying.
There we stand, in command of the powers of darkness.
Don't come near, no time for fear, as devils are cast out and scurrying about.
We plead the blood, and then comes the love of God.
Hugging, sighing, crying, slain, and coming up in Jesus' name, Nairobi!

Obama's Village

In the Bush;
In the Wild;
Under the Net;
Dogs Barking;
Drums Beating;
The Holy Spirit Hovering;
Clash between Good and Evil;
Victory Came;
Never the Same;
Kisumu Africa!

Rosalind Y. Tompkins

The Moon in My Window

The melodic sound of the French language spoken fluently and passionately;
the polite and pleasant smiles and nods;
bon appétit, indeed!
The food so fresh, until you taste the essence of flavor,
as you savor every morsel of fresh pineapples, rice and beans, fish and chicken just killed;
Have your fill!
A place where God is magnified;
a place of joy;
a place of pride, Burundi!

Genocide

Children dying
Mothers crying
Women raped
No escape
Where to hide
It's Genocide!
Jesus died
Shed His blood
Rose again
So we could win
Against all sin!
Help is coming
Letter writing
Outraged sighing
What to do?
It's up to you!
Praying and fasting
Listening and speaking
We won't stop until someone's keeping
Watch over the children of the world.
God Bless the children!

Rosalind Y. Tompkins

A Thousand Hills

Rwanda, the country of a thousand hills;
around and around the mountains as we make our way to the city of tears sown during the years of genocide;
one million died!
Restoration is taking place;
you can see hope on the faces of those who survived the worst and are now looking ahead for the best in spite of the mess of the past.
Rwanda, Rwanda, God is near, have no fear, He does hear your cries.
You will never be the same as you call on the name that is above every name.
Jesus loves you, Kilgali!

ABOUT THE AUTHOR

Rosalind Y. Tompkins has been said to be an icon in Tallahassee, Florida and surrounding areas because of her work with families and communities in crisis. The over twenty-years in recovery former addict founded **Mothers In Crisis, Inc. (MIC)** in 1991. **MIC** is a non-profit, community-based organization comprised of women and men in recovery from drug and alcohol addiction. Through **MIC** she has impacted the lives of thousands of families. She also founded **Turning Point International Church** in 1998.

Rosalind Y. Tompkins is the published author of the books, "*As Long As There Is Breath In Your Body, There Is Hope*", "*Rare Anointing*", and the newly released, "*You Are Beautiful*". She is a prophetic poet who writes and recites poetry and spoken word and has been compared to the likes of Mayo Angelo. She has two CD's of poetry, "*Poems of Life Volumes One and Two*" and three of her poems have been arranged into song on the CD "*The Destiny Project*" by gospel recording artist, Theresa Morton of Atlanta, GA.

The Florida State University graduate has literally branded the Tallahassee and surrounding areas with the now famous trademark, "*As Long As There Is Breath In Your Body, There Is Hope®*"!

With a ready smile, piercing eyes and a warm heart she teaches and preaches in prisons, and pulpits throughout the nation and around the world.

Rosalind Y. Tompkins is also a spiritual Life Coach who helps others fulfill their God given dreams and destinies! Her passion in life is to see lives transformed and activate positive change in others. She is truly a living testimony in the hand of God!

Rosalind Y. Tompkins is available for consultations and speaking engagements. Please contact P. O. Box 5121, Tallahassee, FL 32314-5121, 1-866-430-1050, Ryt2@aol.com, www.rosalindytompkins.com, for more information.